D1553807

CITY OF ROSES

City of Roses

Stories from Girlhood

MARY JANE MOFFAT

John Daniel, Publisher
SANTA BARBARA
1986

Typeset in Baskerville by
Jim Cook Book Design & Typography
SANTA BARBARA, CALIFORNIA

LIBRARY OF CONGRESS CATALOGING-IN-PUBLICATION DATA
Moffat, Mary Jane.
City of roses.
1. Moffat, Mary Jane—Childhood and youth.
2. Portland (Or.)—Biography.
I. Title.
F884.P853M64 1986   979.5′49   [B]   86-19689
ISBN 0-936784-08-3 (PBK.)

Published by
JOHN DANIEL, PUBLISHER
Post Office Box 21922
Santa Barbara, California 93121

We're still trying to get away from Portland, Oregon.
Sign on a San Francisco Beat era cafe

Contents

THE VIEW FROM
RIVERVIEW CEMETERY

A FEW YEARS AGO when my father was still very much alive, I dreamed him dead. In the dream I was myself, a middle-aged widow with grown sons. I was also the girl who grew up roller-skating on the sidewalks of Portland, the City of Roses. I skated down those sidewalks past all the familiar landmarks to the funeral home to say good-by. As I approached the coffin, my father raised up from the satin and beckoned me closer, the way he did when he wanted to tell me a joke. He gave me his pained, Jack Benny dead-pan. He said, "Sit down, kid. This is going to take a long time."

And so it did. Many times in the years surrounding that dream my mother phoned to say, "You'd better come. This may be your last visit with your Daddy. It's real bad this time."

She's not an alarmist; she hates to worry me. So I'd book an airplane ticket and scramble for a substitute for my Lit classes at the University where I teach. I took to keeping a black, packable dress in my closet for a visit to Portland that would end in a funeral.

The dresses kept going out of style. By the time I arrived, the manic energy that infected my father's later years had careened him out of the hospital and back to his bad old ways. He wouldn't go to bed for seven and eight day stretches; he took long mysterious bus trips from their suburb into town— "Puddle City," as he called Portland; he'd prowl all night around their small bungalow by the lake, interrupting one pointless project to start another, from polishing brass to burning soup.

"What brings you home?" he asked, when I showed up for one of these "last visits."

"I was in the neighborhood," I said, setting down my suitcase in the living room.

"Nice of you to drop by. I thought you only came to Portland for funerals." He slipped his horn-rimmed glasses down his nose and scrutinized me. "Such a beautiful daughter I have. It's an honor to have your look in on our little nest."

He gave his lord-of-the-manor gesture to the room, its once-white calcimined walls smudged with cigarette smoke. The living room had become increasingly devoted to his many ailments: a Barca-Lounger near the kitchen alcove where he watched TV at high volume and shouted requests to my mother as she cooked around the corner. Next to his chair, an aluminum TV table piled with ointments for his swollen, scabrous legs that he was supposed to keep elevated but usually kept crossed; a plastic urine bottle under the afghan tossed on the floor; the thermostat turned to 90 degrees because he was always cold; on the burn-scarred leatherette lamp table near his chair, a month of magazines and newspapers, his magnifying glass, hearing aid batteries, and a packet of needles for his insulin injections.

"It may not be much," he said, "but it's home-sweet-home to us. Right, Esther?"

Around the corner, busy at the stove, my mother growled, "Right. Right."

"So how's San Francisco? You promised to send me some *Berkeley Barbs* and you never did."

"You look awful," I said. "How long's it been since you shaved?" When I was a girl, he was so meticulous.

He pushed his glasses back up on the bridge of his nose, gave me another appraising look and said, "You know kid, you're no spring chicken anymore."

I laughed and he gave me a bear hug—I was surprised at the strength he still could put in a hug.

"Thank God you're here," he said. "You're the only one who understands me."

For a little while on these visits I'd be grateful that he hadn't checked out yet. But soon I'd see his terrible temper when crossed, the bruises on my mother's arms where he'd grabbed her in a rage.

"No one ever talks to me," he'd complain, following her from room to room, his own talk never stopping. When she escaped to the bathroom, he'd talk to her through the walls.

She has a peasant's constitution coupled with a cheerful disposition; but he was wearing her down. I'd catch her clapping her palms to her brow, holding her head in her hands. If two days of his relentless presence sent me back to the Bay Area for a week in bed, living with him twenty-four hours a day, month in and out, required stamina I couldn't begin to imagine.

"You've got to get away," I told her the second day of my visit, without having any idea how she could pull off such an escape—I'd already plotted my own and was leaving in the morning.

We were in the kitchen and she was putting up her famous garlic dills, jamming the fresh-picked cukes into the mason jars.

"You know I did run away one night," she whispered slyly. My father, sitting around the corner with the television blaring, was selectively hard-of-hearing—anything to do with him he picked up easily.

"It was one of his door-banging nights and I thought my skull would crack. I just got in the car and checked into a motel down on the highway."

I was thrilled. The notion of his banging doors and shouting, then suddenly realizing there was no one there.

"I hope you stayed two weeks. I hope he was frantic with worry."

"Trouble is," she said, sealing a lid with metal pliers, "I forgot to bring anything to read or any bourbon. I only had a pack of cigarettes and they were gone in no time I was so worried about him."

"So you were back home by dawn's early light."

"A little earlier," she said. "Can you believe? I really missed him."

"Was he glad to see you?"

"Ha! Sweet as pie. For about an hour." She grinned but then she took my hands in hers, hot from the sterilized jars.

"Promise me," she said. "If something happens to me first, you're not to try and take him in. You've had enough troubles. Commit him. Whatever. I won't be here to see it."

"Let's not even think about such a thing," I said, suddenly busy scrubbing the scarred formica. That he might survive her and that I'd be stuck with him was my deepest dread.

"In some ways," she said, suddenly busy herself, "you two are too much alike to ever get along."

The following February she had a stroke. There was no paralysis, but a confusion, a difficulty pulling up the right word in a sentence. "They've put me in this garage," she told me on the phone from her hospital bed."

The day she was released from the hospital, I flew to Portland and found her staring at the burned pots and Augean disorder he'd created in her absence. She put her elbows on the counter and cradled her head in her hands and murmured, "Shit, shit, oh shit, shit, shit."

"Don't worry, I'll take care of her," my father hollered from his Barca-Lounger. And then he asked her to fix him a cup of coffee. "And as long as you're up, be an angel and fetch me the new *Playboy*." To me, he stage-whispered, "She *hides* them."

That night I put her to bed in the small back bedroom so his prowling wouldn't disturb her. I made myself a bed on the living room sofa. Father promised to go to sleep soon and I put a pillow over my head. At 4 a.m. he was still playing his Bessie Smith 78's and had just started burning a batch of bean soup. When I got up to blow out the candles he'd left burning in their brass holders on the mantel, he chuckled and quoted Edna St. Vincent Millay: "My candle burns at both ends..."

Somehow, with "Give Me a Pig's Foot and a Bottle of Beer" playing in the background, this struck me as hilarious. I couldn't stop laughing.

"I love your laugh," my father said. "It's so wicked. What's the matter? Can't you sleep?"

Later that morning while he was in the bathroom, I phoned their doctor. "The only way you'll get Bob into a rest home," he said, "is to take him to court and have him declared incompetent. And I guarantee you that he will rise to the occasion and appear saner than you." He agreed, though, that I had to get my mother out of there.

"But if I leave him here alone, he'll burn the house down."

"Look at it this way," the weary doctor said. "At least he'll just burn himself up."

Two days later when the taxi came to take Mother and me to the airport, Father said, "Good riddance. Now I can have some fun without you two nagging me all day." But he clung to my mother after their good-by kiss. He and I didn't kiss; as I fumbled with the baggage, he gave me a level look that said he understood my gamble. "Take good care of her," he said.

The doctor had arranged for a woman from the Visiting Nurses Association to check on him four times a week and she arrived just as we were leaving. "God damn you," my father shouted at her. "Who needs you?" We drove away to the sight of him waving his cane at her and at some neighbors coming up the walk with a casserole.

"Hurry," I told the cab driver. "We've got a plane to catch." My mother gave me an apalled look. "This is wrong," she said.

I'd never had my mother all to myself before. But as we sat having our drinks each evening in my redwood house on the peninsula, she was disinterested in any subject but him. "As your father would say," began most of her sentences. "I'll pay you for this call," she said as soon as the rates changed and she could speak to him herself. After she hung up, she'd shake her head. "He doesn't sound good," she told me.

"He hasn't for years," I said. "Don't worry." I knew that she held against me in some moral account book every day I kept her in California; and I was torn between wishing he'd let go so she could live and fearing that if he did die she'd never forgive me.

By early May she seemed fairly rested and I found her one morning with her suitcase packed and ready by the door. "He is my husband," she said, with a certainty that awed me.

Two weeks after her return, she telephoned to say that he was in the hospital. "I think this is it. You'd better come."

I took a taxi directly from the airport to the hospital. When I walked into his room, I heard him say hoarsely to my mother as she fussed at his covers, "I want to go home."

I saw immediately that he wasn't going to careen home this time. Even in the wreckage of his last few years, he'd been a handsome man. Now his belly was grotesquely swollen, his blue eyes shone hugely from an emaciated face, a long, scraggly white beard strafed the sheet. I wouldn't have known him if she weren't there.

"All right, Bob, it's home you shall go," my mother said. "I'll talk to the nurse and we'll get your things packed up. And when we get home, I'll fix you a nice supper."

Don't lie to him, I thought. I said, "Go have some lunch. You look like you're ready to drop."

She nodded. His great eyes followed her out the door and he seemed to fall into sleep.

I'd done this to him, I thought; taking her away. I looked out the window to the cement patio under the eaves of his room. A darkness, which at the time I thought was rain, slanted down through the pines. When I looked back at the bed, his eyes were fixed on me. With effort, he lifted his right arm and pointed at me in a slow, punctuating summons. I wasn't sure he knew who I was, but whoever I was, he wanted me closer. I moved into the sphere of his gaze.

He looked at me a long time. He knew who I was.

"I'm going to die," he said.

My tongue started to form placating lies. But he was my old comrade. I felt as if I were inside his eyes now, looking out at me, waiting for me to say something.

"I know," I said. "Try not to be afraid."

He said something else but I wasn't sure I'd heard him right and I brought my face closer to his and he said it again; with some of the old rascal gleam in those haunted eyes, he said, "I'm too young to die."

He lingered for another hour as the sky outside his room turned darker. A nurse told us that Mount St. Helens, fifty miles to the north, had erupted. As a child, I'd picnicked with my parents on its slopes, never dreaming what lay below. My mother and I walked away from his sheeted body and out the hospital automatic doors into an ash storm.

The next day as I waited on the stoop for my mother to lock the front door before we drove to the mortuary to pay him our last visit, I could scarcely see across their street. Wind from the north had layered the dogwood tree with thick ash; the shrubs along the driveway knelt down with soot; motes of ash meandered in the air; I felt them settling in my hair; my teeth felt gritty. Yet, the ordinariness of Mother's fumbling with her keys made it seem as if we were setting off on a Saturday shopping expedition.

The interior of her '68 Buick smelled of stale cigarettes and cracked vinyl. I don't know what there is so sad for me about old car smell. I wished that I could buy her a new one. I wished that I could buy her health, a trip to see her relatives in Finland, some good years. She was only a little older than I am when he fell into the deep depression that made him speak of drowning himself in the lake. She would have been very sad for awhile, but if his death had come when he'd first advertised it, she might have had a good second life.

I started the motor. "We'll have to get the car washed," I

said, peering through the silt on the windshield. Everything was so dirty, everywhere I looked. There didn't seem any way everything could get clean again.

Staring out the window and worrying her thumbs, Mother said, "I want your honest opinion. Should we bury him someplace else?"

"What's wrong with Riverview? The rest of the family is there. He'll be close to his mother." Father had been right. In the last twenty years, I mostly had come home for funerals, real or imminent.

"He always said he hated the view."

I had to hand it to him. He could still make me laugh. "I don't see as it makes much difference, Mother. It's always raining here—there's nothing to see."

She sighed. "Your father used to say that when we died, you'd come up and sell the house in two days, you hate Portland and the rain so much."

"I wish it would rain right now," I said, "and wash away all this ash." Other motorists drove slowly, their lights on as if in a cortege.

At the hospital the day before, I'd heard an old dying woman cry out, "Mama. Mama?" I had to be my mother's mother now, not the frightened child who once found such comfort in her ready arms. I remembered my father's joke about being too young to die. Perhaps it wasn't a joke. Perhaps he'd gone back to childhood and confused me with his mother. I'd sensed no blame in his eyes.

"Why did you only have one child?" I asked, thinking how nice it would be to have a strong, sensible brother or sister right now.

Philosophically, she said, "It wouldn't have made any difference. In every family there's always just one child who takes it all on. No matter how many I'd had, you'd have been that child."

In the gritty parking lot at The Chapel of the Pines, I said, "If you don't mind, Mother, I'll let you off and go do the marketing." I didn't want to see him. Was I afraid that my dream a few years ago might have been a forecast? That he'd sit up and tell me another joke?

Mother didn't argue. I hadn't cut a good figure at the funeral home the evening before. In front of the funeral director, I'd tried to talk her out of having Father embalmed, schoolishly calling it a barbaric custom. "No one wants to see dead bodies," I said, meaning, I suppose, that I didn't want to.

But she has this bulldog expression she uses when she knows she's right. "One more time, *I* want to see him."

I conceded. What did it matter. The funeral director, recognizing where the power lay, turned his full attention to Mother. He got her to go for the $25.00 "Memory Book."

"I imagine, Mrs. Pitts," he said in his sepulchral voice, "that you'll also want the steel liner. It is such a mark of respect."

Mother cast a nervous look in my direction. "How much does it cost?" The director told her, "We have one quite adequate for two fifty."

"Two hundred fifty, he means," I said to my mother. "What does it do?" I asked the director.

He made a steeple with his fingers. "It's guaranteed for one hundred years to protect against seepage." He glanced at me coldly. "You're from California, Mrs. Moffat. We have a different climate here. Here we have a terrible problem with seepage."

I cracked up. "Let him seep," I told that pop-eyed man whose sad occupation it was to gouge the bereaved.

My mother smiled and shook her head. "Mary Jane, sometimes you are so much like your father it slays me."

"That's funny," I said. "Whenever I irritated him, he always said I was so much like you."

I told my mother I'd pick her up in an hour. Roaming the unfamiliar aisles of canned goods and soap powders at the

Safeway was oddly calming. During the war, my father and I
used to market together on Saturday mornings while my
mother worked overtime at her stenographer's job. He used to
brag, "Mary Jane can sniff out a bargain a mile away."

My mother's shopping list that she'd started the morning
before, when I think she still imagined she might bring my
father home, was in itself nostalgic. "T.P." for toilet paper.
"OBJ" for Oh Be Joyful, meaning bourbon. As a child, after
we'd finished the marketing, I used to wait for him outside the
opaque painted windows of the State-controlled liquor
store—the Green Front, he called it—hoping I wouldn't see
any schoolmates.

When he came out with their weekly bottle, he'd say,
"You're the only one who understands me. Your mother..."
And then his list of complaints. Although I adored my
mother, as it seemed did everyone who knew her, he was right;
I did understand him.

I couldn't have articulated it then, but our common griev-
ance was her goodness, her capacity to see us as better than in
our dark, truthful hearts we knew ourselves to be. A country
woman, with a large nose planted on her broad, shiny face,
and a lopsided grin that lighted every room she entered, she
was firmly convinced that she'd been blessed with the most
gifted and handsome husband and daughter that, as she put it,
"God ever put on this earth."

According to my mother, had it not been for a wicked aunt
who cheated him of the chance to go to college, my father
might have been a famous doctor or artist; even, it would seem
when she switched Bob Hope off the radio, a famous
comedian.

"Your father is very much funnier. He could have been..."
Then a heavy sigh, followed by the wisdom of the ages in our
household: "But that's the way the old mop flops."

When Father and I were alone we performed a kind of
corrective surgery on her idealized versions of us.

"I don't think you'd have made a very good doctor," I said,

when he managed to neatly bandage, without ever looking at the wound, one of my many roller-skating scrapes. "Since you can't stand the sight of blood."

"Your mother says you're graceful. Ha! You can't even take a flight of stairs without spraining your ankle."

I was supposed to keep the furniture dusted. One Saturday when I was in fifth grade, we were cleaning the apartment together while Mother worked and I found the letters S L U T fingered in the neglected dust of the veneer coffee table.

"What does that mean?" I asked Father.

"Look it up." He was polishing the dining table with Old English.

I checked the dictionary in his bookshelf. "Daddy!" I protested. I was old enough to understand that I wasn't "a lewd woman."

Slyly, he said, "Look up the second definition."

"A slatternly woman." He had me. Then he gave me a brand new oil-treated dust cloth as a "surprise."

Before we vacuumed, he made a game of lining up the dining chairs in rows, so that the room looked like a Finnish church my mother once had dragged us to. "Now we shall have a meeting," my father intoned, imitating the Finn preacher. I laughed myself silly at Father's version of the sermon which ended, "And if you don't change your unrighteous ways, you will end as seepage, seeping through the earth until the end of time, the most foul *seepage*." Long after I'd left home, he and I could crack each other up in any solemn situation by commenting gravely, "*Seepage*." "You two," my mother would cluck. "Honestly. I don't know what to do with you."

Our games weren't as much fun without the shiver of devilry we felt when, at any moment, she might walk in the door. When I was ten, she left us for a week to tend an ailing sister in Idaho. By the Sunday of this absence we were both so mopey and bored that we skipped church to go to the movies, a wholesome enough double feature with Sonja Henie and

Jane Withers. When we came out onto the sidewalk, the sun was still high in the sky and we decided to walk across the street to the Orpheum where we ate popcorn during the first feature. I was unsettled by a live act performed during the intermission. A woman—could it have been Sally Rand herself?—performed a fan dance. My father watched raptly. I squirmed.

I'm sure, now, that the dance was aesthetic and that Sally Rand wore a body stocking, but after the second feature when we staggered out into the twilight and the nervous neon of Broadway, my father said, "I don't think we'll mention this to your mother." I agreed. We were so far gone by then in our dissolution without Mother to trawl us home for dinner that we went to the Blue Mouse and ate candy bars through a Laurel and Hardy double bill.

By ten, when we caught the streetcar home, my eyeballs felt loose in their sockets. As we often did when we rode the street-car, we pretended not to know each other but after our movie binge I was too tired to play the game where he sat across the aisle and tried to crack me up by making goony faces when the other passengers weren't looking. When he tucked me into bed, he said, "Don't worry. Your mother will be back tomor-row." And I knew we'd both be better soon.

At the Safeway, I stared at the dustcloths and brooms. A woman politely tapped my shopping cart. "Aren't you Esther's daughter?" One of those friendly, Oregon women with a fussy hairset at odds with her sensible shoes, she said, "I recognized you from your pictures."

I wondered if my mother carried around pictures of her middle-aged daughter the way others show off snaps of their grandchildren. "I'm so sorry about your father," the woman said. "How's your mother doing?"

I said, "She's at the mortuary now. I don't think it's quite sunk in yet."

"Bob was difficult these past few years, but when he wanted to, he could be such a charming, funny man."

His sanity act, I thought.

"We all worried so about Esther. Your mother's a wonderful woman."

"I know," I said.

She gave my shoulder a little squeeze and lowered her voice. "I just want you to know, we all think you did the right thing, taking her to California. You really had no choice."

It was either exactly the right thing, or exactly the wrong thing to say. There in the Safeway aisle amid the dustcloths and brooms, I finally cried for my father.

At the Chapel of the Pines, I found my mother sitting alone in the middle of a row of folding chairs in the viewing room. From the doorway, I made myself look at the body.

I saw that the embalmer's art is a cunning one. The belly was no longer distended. Instead of shaving off the straggling beard, the artist had trimmed it neatly, like Hemingway's in his celebrated prime. His head was turned slightly to the right, the chin elevated. The pose was so like the way he cocked his head after making a joke—his Jack Benny dead-pan before he cracked up himself. Even his old brown suit and green tie had taken on an air. My father looked distinguished. Like the man he might have been.

I crossed the hushing carpet and sat beside Mother, taking her hand in mine. "Doesn't he look nice?" she said.

"Yes," I said. And there was no doubt now: he was really dead.

That evening, after I'd warmed up a casserole neither of us could eat, my mother's friends dropped by with more covered dishes and potted azaleas and cut roses. Everyone had a story about trying to get the ash off things. I'd remembered to pick up the OBJ at the Green Front and kept myself busy in the kitchen making drinks, listening to them tell funny stories about my father, stories he often told on himself like the time he answered the door unshaven, without his dentures and in

Mother's old chenille robe. "Won't you come in, my dear," he told the Avon lady. "I've been hoping you'd call."

The liquor loosening her tongue, I heard my mother say, "Sick or well, not a day went by that he didn't make me laugh. How many women can say that?"

I scraped lasagna into the disposer and thought: it isn't enough. I sensed my father disappearing into a blurred cloud of fond anecdotes. Already he was hovering uneasily above the roofline. I wanted to moor his reality to earth a little longer. I had a mind to join the party and remind the guests of the bruises of his thumbprints on the loose flesh of my mother's arms.

But I knew what she would say: "No matter how mean he got, two minutes later he'd make me laugh. It was the sickness talking, not your father."

During his depressed cycle he once said to me, " 'Love thy neighbor as thou love thyself.' Isn't that the stupidest thing you've ever heard?"

I allowed as how if you could only have one rule, I'd always thought that was a pretty good one.

"But what if you hate yourself?" he fiercely asked.

After the guests left, my mother, a little high, sat in his Barca-Lounger. She'd needed the company—I hadn't been much comfort.

"What do you think he did when he took the bus into Portland and stayed so late?" she mused. This was after his depression lifted and he'd begun to love himself to death.

"I expect he went to dirty movies," I said, wiping away the glass rings on the coffee table.

"I'm surprised at you. Why of course he didn't."

"Okay," I said. "He went to the art museum and admired the nudes."

"The art museum closes at five. He didn't get back until way after midnight. He was so gimpy after his legs went bad, I couldn't sleep, thinking he'd been rolled in some gutter."

"He had the right to be what he had to be," I said. "And now you can sleep."

After she'd gone to sleep in the back bedroom that had become hers since her stroke, I set about to exorcise the living room of his sickness. Into the trash went all the medicines and needles and bandages and wilting roses. I found a place in the over-stuffed garage for the stained Barca-Lounger. About 2 a.m. I put on the record player a '78 of Bessie Smith singing "Between 18th and 19th on Chestnut Street" and started to scrub down the walls. Mother called out, "Bob? Bob, please go to bed now."

At dawn I lay down in the maple bed they'd bought as newlyweds and where in the last few years he'd so rarely slept. The headboard still bore the scars of a picture I'd scratched into the wood when, at age three, I'd convalesced in the mysterious blend of their night-time scents. I wondered if over the years they ever had looked at the scratches and understood what I was trying to draw: three stools for three bears.

I couldn't recall either of them ever scolding me for this marring. It was a cheap bed; perhaps they thought they'd buy a new one when the Depression ended. He'd find a job he liked; she'd quit work and stay home and have my sensible brother or sister. He wouldn't go crazy and I'd grow up unquirky; not be me.

My hands smelled of roses and Lysol, the way his hospital room had smelled the day before. It struck me that maybe he wasn't, at that most solemn moment, joking about being too young to die. My mother had always made us feel we were both so full of *possibilities*. Even in middle age, I still fantasy accomplishing something remarkable someday to justify her pride.

I remember that after he'd said he was too young to die, I'd taken his hand. His long fingers felt cool. I remembered him bandaging my cuts, his revulsion at the actual wound. When he lifted my fingers to his lips and I let them stay there, he

hadn't confused me with his dead mother. He knew who I was
and counted on me to understand him.

The day of his burial, a warm Chinook came up from the
southwest to blow away the ash layering the valley. In the
limousine on the way to Riverview, I held my mother's hand.

   She stared out at the houseboats that hugged the riverbank.
"Do you remember how you and your father always wanted to
live in a houseboat?" she asked.

   I nodded.

   "Supposedly they dirty up the river."

   "Seepage," I said and started to giggle. She gave me a blank
look.

   The limousine turned into Riverview. The rhododendrons
were in full bloom, huge globes of pink, cerise, lavender. At
the top of the hill, I helped her out and we walked across the
road from the gravesite to inspect the view.

   It was one of those rare Portland days where from a high
rise of ground you can see mountains in all directions. Only
St. Helen's, fallen down into itself, was obscured by clouds
and ash.

   "I don't see what he was complaining about," my mother
said. "It's a beautiful view."

   "He was joking, Mother," I explained. "The view's not so
good from where he'll be."

   My mother shook her head. "Honestly," she said. "You
two."

HOMAGE TO MISS THAYER

FIRST GRADE! Those lovely lineny books the teacher passed out the first day. I opened mine and saw a smiling family standing on a lawn with a swing outside a white house—just the kind of place where I would have liked to live. There was even a dog. I buried my face in the smell of new paper, wishing to crawl inside and stay forever in that green, sunshiny garden.

From high above my seat in the first row where the teacher stood in a full skirt came her voice: books are not to wipe our noses on. Books are to be read. Tomorrow we will begin to learn to read. Today we will learn how to hold a book and how to turn its pages. We must never touch a book unless our hands are very clean....

And on and on. I felt so downhearted. By tomorrow I was sure the family and their spotted dog would have driven off in the father's black car, lost to me forever. Great slobbery tears fell on my new plaid jumper; my nose ran and I wiped it on the back of my arm.

The voice above me said, didn't I know enough to carry a handkerchief in my pocket? It said I must go to the girl's lavatory and collect myself.

Collect myself? Wasn't I already here?

Those first weeks of 1939 passed into months and by April and my sixth birthday, I still had not learned to read. What I did learn was a runny-nosed sense of wrongness about myself. The high-topped shoes my father insisted I wear for weak ankles marked me as a baby. My green metal lunch box my mother filled with such care every morning before she left for work was wrong; the other children carried their sandwiches to school in paper sacks. My bibbed jumper was wrong. Girls the teacher praised wore pleated skirts with narrow straps that crossed over the backs of their blouses.

25

The young teacher herself wore, day after rainy day, that same full skirt in a nasty shade of reddish brown. As the smallest child, I'd been assigned the first row seat right under where she stood to instruct us. Perhaps I remember the skirt because it was what I saw the most—that and a view of her nostrils shaped like the black spades on my father's playing cards.

"Look and say," she said, as I stared up beyond that curtain of brown at the glossy chart she pulled down like a window shade. Her long wooden pointer circled a collection of lines that was supposed to mean "car." But to me the c was a teacup handle, the a a ball leaning against a wall, the r a flower with its head cut off and one leaf remaining. All together, in no way did they resemble any automobile I'd ever seen.

I still liked the pictures in the book and the smell and feel of the paper; but the story was moving awfully slowly. Instead of the characters disappearing off the page in the car, it seemed to take weeks for Dick to throw the ball to Spot and for Jane to talk about it: Look, Dick, look. See Spot run.

"Do you read aloud to Mary Jane at home?" the teacher asked my mother in an interview about my lack of progress.

My mother assured her that my father read to me almost every night.

"What kind of books?"

"*Treasure Island*," Mother bragged. "*Swiss Family Robinson.*"

"Please ask him to stop," said the teacher gravely. Those books are too interesting. They impede her motivation."

The black marks on the pages of my books became my enemies. I particularly disliked the letter g and others like it that dared to drop below the line, just as at home I had a mad on with certain members of the silverware family. Spoon was a chubby-cheeked child, anxious to please and Knife was a tall guardian knight. But Fork was a cold queen, capable of sudden viciousness. I refused to touch her. "Will she ever learn to eat right?" my father complained when I speared salad into my mouth with a knife.

I "lost" my green lunch box under a juniper bush on the way home from school. I stamped on my plaid jumper and said I would never never never wear it again. More and more, my father said, "I can't stand it when she whines," and left the house, slamming the door behind him.

I asked my mother what "whines" was. She said not to mind, "Your Daddy has a problem with his nerves. But sometimes we both wonder what happened to the nice little girl we used to have."

When called upon to read aloud in class, I made up stories about the family in the primer. Their shiny car had been a gift from a magical boat that last week had arrived in the Portland harbor. (When I had asked my father when we would own a car, he'd said, "When my ship comes in.") I suggested that the reason the ever-smiling mother always stayed home in her apron was because she had a problem with her nerves and couldn't go to work anymore in an office downtown, the way my mother did.

In the midst of these recitations—just as I was warming to my story—the teacher's eyebrows would beetle together and I'd be told to sit down. When I raised my hand to go to the lavatory, the teacher always excused me even though she made the other children wait until recess. I took to spending more and more time in the cool grey stall with its child-sized toilet, contemplating my wrongness to the tune of flushing water.

One afternoon in May one of the girls with the right kind of pleated skirt came to the lavatory to fetch me; my mother had come to visit our class, she told me self-importantly, as if she knew her better than I. I didn't believe her but there my mother was, sitting in the back row behind the tallest boy. I was very proud of her in her smart navy suit and the little hat my father called a pancake—her presence seemed to perfume the chalk-and-eraser air of the classroom with her own special scent of Downtown, a mix of carbon paper and cigarettes and Evening in Paris. I wanted to run and hug her but the teacher told me to take my seat and recite from the lesson of the day in our primer.

The black letters under the picture performed their usual angry act of trying to escape their imprisonment between the lines and I must have performed my usual act of making up some story about the picture, pausing between every word the way the other children did when they read aloud, because the teacher stopped me. I heard her voice above my head say to my mother in the back row, "You see?"

From my bed that night I heard Mother tell Father in her sad-news voice, "The teacher says she's slow. That she may never learn."

I might have remained a victim of the Sight Method of teaching reading then in vogue in the Oregon schools had not my father's "problem with his nerves" worsened. Before the end of the school term, which I was bound to fail, he had to be hospitalized. Mother took me out of school and sent me to spend the summer with an aunt in southern California.

In the fall when I returned, my parents had moved to a flat on upper Broadway near Portland's downtown. I don't know why. Perhaps it was a cheaper rent than the little house we'd lived in on the outskirts. Perhaps it was better for my father's nerves, now that he was working again, not to have to transfer three times on the bus to and from a district I thought was named Hellengon because Daddy always said that he hated living "way out there to hell and gone."

My mother enrolled me in Shattuck school, a block up Broadway from our wood-framed second floor flat. Always an optimist, Mother lied that I would have successfully completed grade 1-A if I'd been able to finish the term at my former school. Until my records arrived, the secretary sent me to the 1-B classroom.

And there I found Miss Thayer.

She was the oldest woman I'd ever seen, with a puff of white hair that caught the light as she handed us our workbooks that first day. She didn't bend over our desks but knelt beside each student as she helped us find our place or fit our awkward fingers around the new slippery pencils; and so I was able to look her full in the face. Her skin reminded me of a bowl my mother treasured on our what-not stand at home: milky and gilded with hundreds of tiny lines that didn't crack the opaline surface. I know, because the second day of class, before she creaked up from her kneeling position beside my desk, I put my hand on her cheek and she let my hand stay there until its curiosity was satisfied.

Unlike my previous teacher, Miss Thayer seemed to be on good terms wth the chalk when she wrote on the blackboard—there was never that terrible screech that used to make my back teeth ache. Miss Thayer often strolled to the window as she taught us, as if she knew what marvelous dances the motes of light performed on her cloud of hair and her pink scalp.

She moved among us—from the blackboard to the window to the coat closet where she helped us with our wraps, as she called them—in dresses of soft material and even softer colors, colors as soothing as her voice: lavender, moss-green, robin's-egg blue.

On rainy days, Miss Thayer wore around her shoulders a frothy piece of cloth that matched her hair. I'd never seen its like and one day I lagged behind, at recess, bold enough to ask her what it was.

"It's a fichu, little Miss. Now hurry out and play before the bars get wet again—this spell of sunshine won't last long."

This struck me as wonderfully strange. Why would a fish need a shoe?

At recess the kids still called me a baby because of my high-top shoes but now I could return to the haven of Miss Thayer's room and its faint scent of violet talc. When she called upon me to read I imagined that the printing said that Dick and Jane were bad children who made their father ner-

vous. If they didn't stop whining and running in the house
the Red Man—a grinning character who often peeked out
from my bedroom curtains at night—was going to come and
take them away. Miss Thayer listened to my recitations with
considerable interest it seemed to me; at least she shushed the
titters of my classmates and always let me finish.

One warm Indian summer Friday afternoon I was startled
to see my mother appear in the classroom door just as I was
collecting my wrap to go home. In low and anxious tones she
spoke to my teacher about my father: something about a
breakdown and the state hospital in Salem. Daddy was always
complaining about being broke, which I never believed
because he looked all in one piece to me; but now maybe it
was really true. A picture came into my mind of him all alop,
like a puppet with its strings cut.

The next thing I knew I was sitting beside Miss Thayer in
her car, rubbing my palms against the flannely upholstery as
we drove to the country near Gresham. We walked through a
small orchard to her house and she must not have been so very
old for she lifted me easily to pick a bright green apple from a
tree. I bit into its hardness and felt a tiny thrill of pain. When I
looked down at the white meat I saw a drizzle of blood and my
first lost tooth. Miss Thayer and I laughed.

She lived with an even older woman—perhaps her mother
or a sister, I don't remember. They seemed to enjoy each other's company very much and mine as well. In fact, I remember
little of those two days in the country except eating wonderful
food that the other woman prepared, the kind of food that
takes all day to simmer and stew; and in the mornings home-
made bread smeared with apple preserves; collecting wild
grasses with Miss Thayer and watching minnows in a creek
and brightly asking if they wore shoes, knowing full well they
didn't, but pleased at my joke.

But something else must have happened that week-end. On
Sunday afternoon when my mother met me at the bus station
downtown and we walked hand in hand up Broadway, the

neon signs were just jittering on. These bright letters were no longer mysterious enemies. They were simply signals that told me what sounds my lips should make. P: puh, puh, puh—Paramount! M—Mickey Mouse. Sam's Grill. Shoes Repaired. All the way home I read the world to my mother.

AMONG THE BOOKS

AFTER MY GRADE 1B teacher took me home over a weekend and taught me to read by the phonics method, I began my life among the books. In 1940 we moved to a gloomy apartment on Portland's northwest side where I spent many hours alone. My mother promised that next year, when times got better, she'd quit her job. We'd move across the river to a house with a lawn and a swing and a dog. There I'd have playmates and presumably my real childhood would begin. While I waited I found solitude delicious as long as I had something to read.

I was hungry for longer words to move my lips around than the slow prose of my second-grade primer—Ann and Tom had replaced Dick and Jane but weren't a whole lot more fun. My parents owned few hard-cover books and they were dry fodder; *Elbert Hubbard's Scrapbook* whose musty observations made me sneeze; two volumes of *The Decline and Fall of the Roman Empire* with yellowing pages falling loose from the spine; a text on phrenology with illustrations of skull types as they determine character; Gregg's *Business Shorthand*; a numerology book my father had researched to bestow the eight lucky letters of my given name; and a history of my maternal grandparents' homeland called *Finland, The New Nation*.

Although Mother liked to show that book to visitors, I doubt she ever read it. I never saw her sit down to read anything much beyond *The Oregon Journal* with a highball when she came home from her stenographer's job downtown. Devoted to the cartoon strip Snuffy Smith which she always saved for last, she'd rattle the ice dregs in her glass, declare "Time's awastin'," and get on with her chores—which she kept at until late at night when she ironed the fussy pinafores she liked to dress me in—and that I hated.

Father was a reader. On his way home from work he'd stop

at the rental library or the corner drugstore and make straight for his overstuffed chair to lose himself in whatever had caught his eye on the racks, often one of the twenty-five cent pocket books, then just becoming available. On my hands and knees on the carpet, I pretended to be reading the funnies; but I was eyeing his latest title with greed in my heart.

The next afternoon I let myself into our third floor apartment with the key I wore on a string around my neck and read whatever he'd been reading the night before: *Tobacco Road* (putting my finger over the *hells* and *damns* to avoid sin) or a Raymond Chandler mystery.

I still can almost taste those nougaty afternoons curled in father's chair with the only sounds the occasional clank of the elevator cage rising and falling in its shaft or the pigeons muttering in the light well outside our bathroom. And how vividly I remember particular books like *The Story of Mrs. Murphy*, by some forgotten author—Mr. Murphy was a drunk and Mrs. Murphy was booze, my introduction to metaphor.

One evening, wild to get my hands on the copy of *Appointment in Samarra* my father was reading, I asked him how he picked out his books. Although I didn't always understand everything in his selections, they never bored me. How could he know a book was going to be good before he'd read it?

"I just look for lots of white space," he said.

"White space?"

"Dialogue. People talking back and forth. I know it won't take long to read if there's lots of white space. The superintendent tells me he caught you riding the elevator again."

Twice I'd had to be rescued when my playing with the buttons stalled the elevator between floors. "You know I've got a sprained ankle," I said. I should have known better than to interrupt his reading.

"That child can't take a flight of stairs without turning her ankle," my father sighed to no one in particular and went back to John O'Hara's white space.

Father was right. Along with being drastically undersized for my age, I was poorly coordinated, always falling down. Afternoons alone with father's books were even sweeter because they were a reprieve from the after-school deadball games in the school yard. In my pinafore and Shirley Temple hairbow, I was an easy target and spent most of the game in prison behind the lines, frantically waving my arms in pretense that I wanted out. I used to pray for rain so I could go home and read. In Portland, prayers for rain are almost always answered.

In my second grade Sunday school class, I gave an unsolicited book report on *Of Mice and Men* which I'd found ever so much more interesting than that week's Bible verses. On Monday night the kindly nun—we attended High Episcopal then—telephoned my mother to warn her of my inappropriate literary interests.

Mother thanked Sister for her concern but told her, "We're just grateful she can read at all...her 1A teacher said she was slow." After she'd hung up she asked me if I should be reading "anything you can lay your hands on."

"But it's a good story," I protested. "You should read it," and I told her all about how half-witted Lennie accidentally killed the girl and how then his friend George had to kill him to save him from the angry mob. It was sad but not mean like the Bible story we were supposed to read about Abraham being all set to kill his own little boy to make God happy.

"I never held much with that story myself," Mother said. For a brief time thereafter Father kept his books in his top bureau drawer underneath his handkerchiefs; but nothing further was said about my reading habits.

So I continued to read anything I could lay my hands on, exercising no discrimination beyond a story holding my interest. I didn't reject the Bible entirely but preferred the New Testament to the Old where my sympathies always seemed to lie with the wrong person. Lot's wife, for instance. Who wouldn't have looked back to see the city she was getting away from?

I particularly liked the story of Mary and Martha. Sitting at the feet of Jesus listening to his stories instead of fussing in the kitchen, Mary was, I felt, a reader like me. My father's mother lived with my uncle and his wife in the apartment above us and Grandma dropped in often to wonder why I wasn't helping in the kitchen.

"Oh, she's down among the books," my mother said, meaning I was in my bedroom reading.

Grandma thought I should be learning to tat tea towels and darn and was horrified that I didn't even know how to light our gas stove.

Once I heard her complain to my father, "Her mother is giving Mary Jane absolutely no training. What will she do when she gets married?"

Father sighed. "The one time she tried to light the stove she singed off her eyelashes. Anyway, she can read. If she ever does get married, she'll be able to read a cookbook."

"To her maid?" Grandma said drily. Listening from my bedroom, I knew that Marthas were necessary to this world but I hoped that when I grew up I wouldn't have to do their chores.

When I turned eight, I was allowed to take the streetcar downtown by myself and I neglected my own chores as often as possible to visit the three story library, grand as a stone cathedral, on Tenth and Yamhill. The first day I walked up the marble steps to apply for a card, I was stunned by the notion that all the books in the world must be in this hushed building; and that soon I would be able to lay my hands on any and all of them.

After I'd filled out the form, the librarian at the main desk typed out a card for me.

"The children's library is over there," she said, pointing to a smallish room with low tables and chairs.

I looked at my card: "Children's Library" was stamped on it in sickening baby-blue block letters.

"I want a regular card," I said. "I don't like children's books."

"You may apply for an adult's card when you are twelve," she said turning back to her typewriter.

"But my father lets me read anything I want in *his* library!" I argued, transforming Daddy's five-shelf narrow veneer bookcase into an oak-panelled sanctuary.

"And just what kind of books do you enjoy reading in your father's library?" the woman asked, giving me a good lookover for the first time. At eight, I was about the size of a five-year-old, my hairbow barely clearing her counter.

Oh-oh, I thought, remembering the Sunday School uproar over *Of Mice and Men*. "Well, I'm awfully fond of *Elbert Hubbard's Scrapbook*," I said. "And *The Decline and Fall of The Roman Empire* is pretty good."

She pulled at the bun at the nape of her neck and shook her head. "Why you poor child," she said and took me by the hand and led me to the Children's Room. Together we walked among shelves bathed in late afternoon sun from the tall mullioned windows as she pointed out titles like *Heidi* and *A Girl of the Limberlost* and *Ramona* and *A Sweet Girl Graduate*.

"I realize that you are an advanced reader," she said gravely. "If after a month you find nothing here that interests you more than that tiresome Elbert Hubbard, come and see me and I will see about arranging special privileges."

Bless her. For of course I found that the room was not so small after all and that books written for children offered another perspective on the world than what I was getting at home reading *God's Little Acre* and *Butterfield 8*.

The Second World War had begun and although my father got a higher paying job as a pipe-fitter in the shipyards than his previous sales-clerk work, we were "frozen" in our dark five-room apartment and the dream of a house across the river where I could have a dog was, like so much else for so many people during those years, suspended. My own small but real heartbreak at not getting my promised dog was assuaged by the animal books in the Children's Library.

I felt every beating endured by *Beautiful Joe,* a mongrel dog much abused by his succession of masters; I ran through the bracken with faithful *Lassie.* I tracked lions in Africa with Osa Johnson in her *I Married Adventure* (a more promising metaphor than *The Story of Mrs. Murphy*).

One evening my mother came home to find me in inconsolable tears, all my chores undone: the furniture undusted, the newspapers unstacked, the dishes from our hurried breakfast still in the sink. My father's youngest brother was a Marine and the newspapers had reported a terrible battle in the Pacific that day in which our troops had suffered tremendous losses.

Mother tried to soothe my sobs as I lay on the day bed in the dining room, my latest children's library book on the floor. "I know you're worried about Uncle Raymond," she said. "No," I wailed. "Black Beauty died."

So totally did I enter the invented worlds of novels that when I finished one I was always surprised to find I was still stuck in the American Apartments on the corner of 21st and Johnson in Portland, Oregon U.S.A. where nothing interesting ever seemed to happen. The real world was not our dingy neighborhood with its taverns and little shops that sold used comic books or dusty greeting cards; or school and those hateful deadball games and my arithmetic class where I couldn't comprehend the principle of borrowing in subtraction but took from whichever column seemed to have the most to spare—as I noticed our relatives did from each other.

And the real world was especially not my parents' arguments about his family that I heard after I was in bed, quarrels with no resolution except for a hurled dish or a slammed door followed by silence so empty I heard the mice rustling in the baseboards, like a row of dot, dot, dots that read "To be continued tomorrow."

Concerned that I was alone so much immersed in books,
Mother decided I should take lessons after school. Lessons
would spice me up and help me make friends. Most of the
other children at Couch Elementary School were Chinese and
attended Chinese school after the deadball games. Brightly, I
suggested that I too go to Chinese school.

"The next thing you'd know, she'd be going home with
them," Father growled at the dinner table.

I would have liked nothing more—I was dying to see how
my classmates lived in those storefronts with painted-over
windows down by the railroad station.

"That wasn't what I had in mind," Mother said. "I've
taken out a membership for you at the Multnomah Athletic
Club. You can learn to swim and you'll meet some nice children from the Heights."

"Are you trying to send us to the poorhouse?" Father said,
slamming down his fork. "You'll turn her into a snob—pretty
soon she'll think she's too good for us."

But Father was saved both from the poorhouse and my
turning uppity. My first swimming lesson at the Multnomah
Club I almost drowned and refused to return. Next, Mother
signed me up for art lessons at the Museum where I charcoaled
sketches of ill-proportioned dogs which I tore up in tears. For
a few weeks I studied ballet. When I practiced at home, the
tenants in the apartment below us pounded on the ceiling
with a broom handle—the conclusion of my tour jeté particularly enraged them. And even Mother had to admit that the
headaches Father suffered during my brief struggle with the
violin were justified.

And so I was allowed to go happily back down among the
books. My literary pastures grew even greener when at nine I
discovered fairy tales. Ever since I'd received a copy of Kings-
ley's *The Water Babies* as a prize for Sunday School attend-
ance, I'd had no use for fairy tales, thinking they were full of
smarmy characters like Mrs. Do-As-You-Would-Be-Done-By.

But one weekend I was visiting a small-town older cousin

who was trying to include me in her gang's marble game, a game I couldn't seem to grasp. "You don't know how to play *anything*," she snapped. In grief and shame—for she was quite right—I fled inside and found my way to my uncle's unpromising bookshelf. There among dusty back issues of *Washington Hatchery News*, I found *Grimm's Fairy Tales.*

My cousin probably thought I was sulking when the rest of the week-end I ignored her pleas to come and play. I wasn't; I just couldn't stop reading these stories. In some ways the tales were as mysterious and violent as my father's books, full of grotesque creatures and strange curses inflicted on innocents. Their dreamlike quality resembled the nightmares I sometimes suffered; but in the tales the curse was always lifted and the bad creatures sent to some dreadful fate.

All that rainy winter, under the pleased eye of the librarian, I checked out fairy tales. They took my mind off my worries. My natural expression seemed to be a frown, for my teachers often asked me what I was worried about and once a man stopped me on the street and said, "Little girl, you look like you're carrying the weight of the world on your shoulders. What's wrong?"

I wasn't conscious that I was brooding—everything I fretted about had the same weight. Would my father get sick again? He now spent all day Sunday in bed, not sleeping but staring at the wall. Would the elevator I still sneaked rides in one day just keep going through the sixth floor and into the sky with me inside the cage? Would LeRoy Johnson, the blond boy I liked at school, write something mean in my slam-and-compliment book? Would I ever turn pretty like the pastel princess in the illustrated Grimm's?

I worried about the war. Not about my uncle in the Marines—he wrote such boring letters about how much he hated Spam that I couldn't imagine him in any danger. The uncle who lived in the apartment above us was an air raid warden who was supposed to go around the neighborhood checking people's blackout curtains; but I knew that he spent most of his rounds in the Silver Moon Tavern up the street drinking beer. I was sure that some window in the neighborhood was leaking light while Uncle Henry was enjoying his escape from his pruney wife and Grandma. The Japanese would bomb us. Worse, Japanese soldiers would parachute onto our building's roof and handily take the elevator down to the third floor where they'd stick a bayonet through our front door. The soldiers would look like the streetcar posters of Tojo, his canines dripping blood, that warned "Loose Lips Sink Ships." *Banzai*, they'd scream as the door gave way and Father would just lie in bed staring at the wall....

Part of my distress about the war stemmed from guilt. Or if not guilt, unease about one of the volumes in our home bookshelf. Nurtured on Norman Rockwell posters of The Four Freedoms, I was fiercely patriotic, stealing quarters from my Sunday School Lenten mite box to contribute to the war bond collections each week at school. I loved Franklin Roosevelt, who'd been President since before my birth and who spoke to us each week on the radio, calling us his friends in his fireside chats. Indeed, one of the ways I motivated myself to stop reading after school and straighten the apartment before my parents arrived was to fantasy that Eleanor and Franklin Roosevelt might drop by and notice that the chair rungs were undusted. Might they also notice Mother's book on the shelf, *Finland, The New Nation*? Finland recently had sided with Germany. How could I tell them that although I was half-Finnish, I wasn't a traitor? My Japanese classmates had disappeared last year—would Mother and I be hauled away to some camp?

One Saturday afternoon I went alone to the movies to see *Abbott and Costello Meet the Zombies*. The newsreel showed a scene of American soldiers burning books with swastikas on their covers in pyres on the street. They must be raiding homes for suspicious materials, I thought. In panic I ran home and found my mother in the basement laundry room pulling socks through the wringer and told her we had to get

rid of her book on Finland before the soldiers came and found
it.

Mother put her arms around me and told me I musn't be
ashamed of being Finnish. If I'd read her book, she said, I
would understand that the only reason the Finns signed that
pact with the Germans—bad as they were—was because they
knew how cruel the Russians were. I was shocked when she
said, "Really. The only thing worse than a bad German is a
good Russian." We were traitors after all.

She flatly refused to get rid of the book so I hid it myself
behind the unused Murphy bed in my room. If the soldiers
came, I reasoned, I would tell them I was in the habit of
reading anything I could lay my hands on and that I'd found
it in a garbage can. That at least would put mother in the
clear.

Mother must have sensed how upset I was because that
night she sat on the edge of my bed and said, "I didn't mean to
say the Russian people are bad. Just their leaders."

"They're our allies," I chided, refusing to look at her.

"I know. You yourself contain Russian blood."

"I do?" I sat up in bed and envisioned myself sturdy in a
babushka, wielding a scythe against golden wheat.

"Don't tell your grandma—I doubt she'd understand."
(Grandma liked to brag that one of *her* ancestors joined the
Boston Tea Party. Mother hadn't endeared herself to Grandma
when she said she'd heard they let prisoners out of jail to
throw that tea.)

Said Mother, her voice low, "When your great-grandmother
was sixteen she was lady-in-waiting at the court of Czar
Nicholas II. But she got pregnant and was sent back to Finland in disgrace. Your grandfather was the baby."

This was the steamiest stuff I'd ever heard. "Who was the
father?" I whispered.

"Let's just say he was someone very important."

The Czar! I was descended from royal blood. This seemed
to explain a lot about why I wasn't suited for a childhood

cooped up in an apartment in Portland, Oregon. (Years later,
my mother told me she meant to imply the mad monk Ras-
putin as my putative ancestor.)

But I did realize then that she meant my somber Methodist
grandfather was a bastard. From father's books, I dimly knew
what a bastard was although I didn't know yet the actual
mechanics of how one was produced. I felt a sort of thrilling
confusion about all this. One day I'd lay my hands on enough
books to understand everything.

I think now that I read my father's books partly as a way of
understanding him. A tall man with dark curly hair and a
striking widow's peak, he kept changing on me. One year
he'd be terribly thin, handsome as Robert Taylor; and a few
months later he'd put on fifty pounds and resemble Laird
Cregar who played movie villains. When he read amusing
books like *Barefoot Boy With Cheek* or *Lost in the Horse
Latitudes* I could count on good times playing word games
with him while he stirred spaghetti sauce, his cigarette con-
stantly burning in the ashtray on the kitchen window ledge.
He had a wonderfully wicked laugh. When he read Mary
Lasswell's *Suds in Your Eye*, he laughed at least once a para-
graph; and then I knew I'd talk him into a walk later to
Washington Park to push me on the swings.

But when he brought home grim books like the Studs Lon-
igan novels, it meant his own emotional weather had darkened, as if he were drawn to stories of lives shabbier and
meaner than ours to reassure himself. I learned to predict the
times when he'd make snide jokes about my mother's
farmerish walk or my stringy hair, or linger at the beer parlor
on the way home to play the punchboard. Mother would give
her Baltic sigh as dinner grew cold. "It could be worse," I told
her. I knew. I read his books.

In 1943, my tenth summer, my mother grew sick of "you two
sad-sacks," as she called us. There wasn't much she could do

about Father's lying abed all week-end but she told me, "You are not going to spend all summer in this apartment reading."

I groaned, fearing she had something horrible in mind like horse-back riding lessons—Black Beauty aside, I was terrified of horses in the flesh. I'd been wanting to buy some sixty-cent Nancy Drew mysteries that I couldn't get at the library so I suggested that I get a job picking hops as some of the kids at school planned to do.

"You'd last about ten minutes picking hops," my father said with a snort.

"I did not raise you to be a field hand," Mother said. She proposed enrolling me in drama classes at the Portland Junior Civic Theater.

"That's right," said Father. "Get her out of a dark apartment into a dark theater. How much is this going to cost?"

With my usual bright outlook, "It'll just rain all summer anyway," said I.

Memory should tell me if it rained a lot that summer, because I had to take the streetcar to the southwest side; but the minute I walked into the cool greyness of the Civic Theater with its pink masks of tragedy and comedy hanging on either side of the proscenium, I didn't care if I ever went out into sunshine again. The grownups bustling about seemed like characters from Father's jolliest books—the costume mistress who always had a cigarette hanging from her lips but never flecked an ash on a garment; the tiny Russian dance instructor who wore only purple; the stagehands whistling backstage as they sawed and painted flats; and Miss Zamvill, the drama coach who wore a lorgnette around her neck on a silver chain and gave stern directions in a buttery voice. They all moved their hands extravagantly as they talked, called each other darling and treated us children like delicious, miniature adults. ("Now darling, start your gesture from your belly-button and sweep your arm past your little bosom into the sky beyond.")

Miss Zamvill cast me as the Irish cook in a play called *The*

Dyspeptic Ogre (the ogre required a diet of children but they upset his stomach). The cook was a marvelous role, probably fool-proof. She helped the captured children escape from their cages and wheedled the ogre into believing a vegetable dish was "a plump ten-year old lad stewed to a tender turn." It reminded me of the way my mother sometimes sweet-talked my father into doing what was best for him.

To catch the cook's accent I sat through four showings of *Going My Way* and borrowed a brogue from Barry Fitzgerald. When on opening afternoon the audience laughed at all my lines, my mother's dogged efforts to unearth some hidden talent in her bookish daughter were repaid. The theater was books made visible. Even better than reading them was bringing them to life.

As I continued to act in both children and adult productions at the Civic Theater, the solitude of my reading gave way to an intense rehearsal schedule. I was, as they say in the theater, a quick study and I whispered their lines to other actors when they forgot them. A shameless egoist, I wanted to play all the parts and often did before the mirror at home.

One morning before my mother left for work, in the bathtub I practiced the balcony scene from *Romeo and Juliet* while she made up her face in the mirror over the sink:

O swear not by the moon, the inconstant moon . . .

Mother put down her mascara brush and said, "No one will ever take that away from you." I was puzzled then by her remark. She acted as if I were gaining something precious that she and my father had been denied. All I was aware of was that I was having a good time.

In January 1947 I entered high school. The mid-year program was phased out and we students who'd entered first grade in January were obliged to complete our freshman year by June. Double sessions of solid courses—algebra as mysterious to me as subtraction once had been, my equally mysterious new popularity, along with amateur theater and professional radio work, left me less time to prowl the apartment for Father's latest books.

Father, who had neglected to keep me from reading the randiest books available in the 1940's, now met my dates at the door as if he were the guardian of the last vestal virgin in a temple surrounded by infidel marauders. While I pinned the requisite gardenia corsage on my pink organdy, he questioned the date who'd delivered it about the year, make and model of the car I'd be transported in, the condition of the tires. I tried hard to keep a straight face—Father himself had never learned to drive. "And I want her home right after the dance. No parking out at Rocky Butte or on Council Crest, young man."

I was both mortified for my blushing date and amazed. How did Father know the best necking spots?

He needn't have worried. The novels of the era, shocking as they may have been to my second grade Sunday School teacher and other moral watchdogs, never suggested that anything but sordid or tragic consequences resulted from sexual dalliance. Indeed, they had the opposite effect: the idea of anything beyond the most tentative backseat forays scared me stiff. In my sophomore year, a superb piece of trash passed among my giggling girlfriends. So unsettled was I by the featherings in my groin aroused by reading *The Sheik* that I concluded: if an absurd story of an intelligent woman happily held captive in an Arab's tent exerted such power over me, I'd do well to do considerably more reading before succumbing to the temptations of late evenings at Rocky Butte or Council Crest.

My extracurricular life in high school was so rich that by my senior year I knew I'd have to settle down and go to college if I wanted some knowledge beyond that offered by my scattered readings of novels. No one in my family had ever been able to go beyond high school, and my mother, especially, dearly wanted this for me.

My grades were good but not outstanding. As it was, I

think my teachers may have been lenient about my many
absences for radio work, my lack of attention in morning
classes when I'd been up late the night before rehearsing or
performing in amateur plays. The summer between my junior and senior years I'd played Juliet at the Shakespearean
festival in southern Oregon. This brought me some attention
in the local papers and perhaps minor celebrity prompted my
teachers to give me A's when I deserved B's, B's when I
deserved C's. All I know is that I learned little in most of my
high school courses. The class work and the dry texts seemed
like tedious interruptions of the far more dramatic lives in
Father's novels and my life on stage, at sorority meetings,
dances at the country club, and slumber parties with my
girlfriends where intense philosophical discussions surrounded
such issues as: was Sally Sue Heffernan justified in going out
with Tuffy Moorehead when Tuffy was practically pinned to
Earlina Johnson?

Cavalierly, throwing my fate to some arbiter outside my
control, I applied to only one school, Stanford. "The most
expensive one you could have chosen," Mother gasped.

I recklessly saw the gamble as between escaping to the eter-
nal sunshine of California and being stuck in rainy Portland
the rest of my life. Whatever the gods decree, I told myself.

The Stanford Admissions Committee must have given
some credit for extracurricular activities. I'd like to think I
wrote a bang-up admissions essay but all I remember from
that piece of prose is working in the term *esprit de corps*, not
quite sure what it meant.

I was accepted. Mother said she'd find a way to borrow the
money for my tuition. Father embarassed me by saying over
and over, "You're a lucky, lucky girl." Grandma said, "Maybe
she'll find a rich husband." But she wondered aloud what he'd
think when he discovered I didn't even know how to light a
stove.

For a going-away present Father gave me a Webster's *Col-*

legiate Dictionary and the admonition: "Just don't do anything you wouldn't want to tell me about." At Stanford, in a
freshman psychology class, I read of an experiment by Dr.
Clara Davidson in which infants left to choose their own
foods without interventions, over a period of time crawled
their way to dishes that resulted in a perfectly balanced diet. I
guessed that until then, my own eclectic reading had given
me—one random taste leading to the savor of its sour or sweet
counterpart—all the imaginative calories I needed.

But when I was assigned the thick brown volume of
Burns's *History of Western Civilization,* I discovered how
truly little I knew. No one in Sunday School or high school
had ever bothered to tell me that centuries before Judaism and
Christianity humans had worshipped a virgin goddess, had
believed in a redeemer. Suddenly I was deeply troubled.
Maybe the faith I'd learned at the Episcopal church on 19th
and Gleason wasn't infallible.

I wrote my father of my troubles. Was religion perhaps just
nice poetry that from the beginning of time helped people get
through a hard life?

He wrote back, "It seems a goddamned shame that your
mother is paying all this money for you to lose your religion.
What are you, getting uppity on us? Can't you drop the
course? Grandma wants to know if they offer Home
Economics."

I wrote Father that Western Civ was a required course, but
not to worry. I didn't tell him that his drugstore novels had
been a fine prerequisite. For me, at just the right time and at
just the right age, I began to learn how to read books.

SIXTEEN UNDER THE STARS

"But soft, what light through yonder window breaks?"

ON OPENING NIGHT of the 1949 Oregon Shakespearan Festival in Ashland, right on cue, I slipped through the curtains and dreamily rested my hand on the balcony railing. The spotlight caught my blonde hair in its beam and I heard the audience give a little gasp of pleasure as Romeo proclaimed from the apron stage below, in a voice like flowing velvet, "It is the east, and Juliet is the sun."

I wasn't feigning adolescent rapture when I trebled out to the starry night, "Romeo, Romeo, wherefore art thou Romeo?" In my very soul, I truly was the fourteen-year-old daughter of the feuding Capulets, sighing to the vine-covered garden walls on a balmy Mediterranean evening in the fifteenth century. At the same time, and just as firmly, I was sixteen-year-old Mary Jane Pitts of Portland, winner of a state-wide contest for the Juliet role, in love with the actor who played Romeo, with my thrilling vocation, and, to a considerable degree, with myself.

I fixed my gaze on the banners fluttering above the stone wall that surrounds the outdoor Elizabethan theater and put pure heartbreak in my voice: "What's in a name? That which we call a rose by any other name would smell as sweet." I felt I understood and fully conveyed the tragedy in the lines, for at twenty-four the dazzling, muscular actor who played Romeo was far too old for me. Alas, when summer ended, our love too was doomed.

"Deny thy father and refuse they name," I plead in my soliloquy to the stars. The roar of a DC6 making its descent into the nearby Medford airport broke the spell. No longer was the audience in a renaissance Italian garden—I sensed the theatergoers shifting in their folding chairs, pulling on lap robes and sweaters as the last of the day's warmth disappeared into the brown folds of the Siskiyous. "Or if thou wilt not," I shouted, "I'll no longer be a Capulet." I cringed at the fish-wife shriek of my voice—my acting experience before this was in a 250 seat enclosed theater with excellent acoustics.

But soon the airplane landed and that special silence fell that means an audience is truly listening.

Now I felt that if I could just get through the scene when Juliet learns from her nurse that her cousin Tybalt is dead and Romeo, his murderer, is banished, all would be well. The cords scene called for an arpeggio of emotions—anger, grief, passionate longing for her wedding night—harder for me to orchestrate than the wistful tenderness of the Juliet first in love. Juliet's nurse resolves her anguish by bringing her a corded ladder that Romeo will mount to Juliet's bedroom so the two can consummate their love.

In rehearsals of the cords scene, Harvey, the play's director, who'd played a small role in the New York production star-ring Katherine Cornell, explained how "Kit," as he called the famous actress, had rendered Juliet's emotional conflict. He told me how she tossed her head (tossing his own head), how she'd torn the bodice of her gown, how her throaty voice could project the merest whisper to the back rows.

Politely, I told Harvey that wasn't the way a fourteen-year-old girl sounded to me. (Privately, I felt sorry for "Kit," an old woman in her forties, trying to portray Juliet.) I myself used Stanislavsky's method of sense-memory to get back to the way I'd felt two years ago when I was a freshman and Billy, the cutest boy in the sophomore class, had asked me to wear his Hi-Y pin.

Harvey clutched his balding blond temples. "This is Italy, not Portland. Juliet's ripened early under the Mediterranean sun—at fourteen she's sexually mature. If she'd lived to twenty, she'd have been a toothless hag. Sweetheart, try and get just a teensy bit more lust in your voice. And pro*ject*."

Poor Juliet, I thought on opening night. Better off dead than living to twenty with no teeth and a courtyard full of screaming children. Happily, after the staged drama had ended, I wouldn't be lying cold on a bier in a festering tomb with a dagger in my heart alongside Tybalt and the other family corpses. I loved drama but real life—at least this summer—was far better. As we had every night after rehearsals, tonight Romeo and I would drive to the diner on the highway and drink chocolate milkshakes so thick the sweetness wouldn't slurp through the straws.

Last June in auditions when I'd first set eyes on Romeo, I wasn't impressed. With his carefully curled forelock of auburn hair, he was too slick for my taste, too conscious of his gestures and dazzling smile. But after we were cast as the star-crossed lovers and folks went out of their way to tell us what a handsome couple we made, I more or less willed myself to fall in love, considering it almost a vocational duty to bring credibility to my performance. And how gorgeous he looked in his green tights tonight, proclaiming his love under a spotlight moon while the real moon bathed the theater with its more distant affection.

After our milkshakes, Romeo and I always sat awhile outside the college dorm where I boarded, exchanging fluttering kisses in the front seat of his Nash coupe. A war veteran, a seasoned man of twenty-four, he never made a move beyond those honeyed kisses. On his staticky radio, the local station played "But Baby, It's Cold Outside" ("I really must go, but...") and before midnight, even though the dorm stayed open until one, he'd always sit up, slick back his hair and say, "Well kid, gotta get my beauty sleep." Which I thought rather spoiled the poetry of the moment.

I always ran my tongue across his eyelids before I whispered, "Parting is such sweet sorrow," and drifted up the stairs to my second-floor room to put "The Moonlight Sonata" on the record player and moon awhile myself over this magical summer. I'd left the rains of Portland behind. I was Juliet and I was the sun.

The cords scene did go well that August opening night. At

least I felt more in control of my wavering voice than I ever
had in rehearsals. Perhaps the steady Southern Oregon sunshine and my steady diet of kisses was ripening me a bit. In the
final scene when I lay on the bier and Romeo threw his grief-
stricken body over mine, I felt the heat of his sex against my
own and slipped my tongue between his teeth for his final kiss
(to test his concentration, I teased him later). Through my
shroud, he pinched my thigh and we both started to break up
but stifled our bubbles of laughter and managed to look, our
bodies flung together in a last embrace, quite dead.

The Prince of Verona entered, scolded all our friends and
families and summed up the tragedy:

> For never was there a story of more woe
> Than this of Juliet and her Romeo.

The audience applauded long and hard, especially when
Romeo and I and the snowy-haired scholar, who was built
like Mussolini and played my nurse in grandly bawdy style,
took our bows. My eardrums, my whole body reverberated
from the clapping when the founder of the festival reached up
over the fender of the stage and presented me with a bouquet
of long red roses. I plucked one stem and, bowing in homage,
gave it to my nurse; and took another and chucked the bud
under Romeo's chin, milking a good two more minutes'
applause from the opening night crowd. Well, that certainly
was an inspired touch, I told myself, and made a deeply hum-
ble curtsey.

The strolling musicians in Elizabethan garb piped the
strains of "Greensleeves" on their recorders and flutes and the
audience began to drift toward the gates of the old chautauqua
shell that had inspired the founder to build a Shakespearean
theater on this knoll above Lithia Park. In the second row I
spied my parents, still gazing awestruck at the stage. They'd
brought my grandmother down on the bus from Portland and
I blew them all a kiss, meaning I'd see them later. Mother
nodded and blew me back a kiss; Father made a circle with his

thumb and index finger and Grandma shuffled in her oversize purse for some lost object.

A line of smiling playgoers made their way to the steps that mounted the stage. I took a deep breath to prepare for my second performance of the evening, a role I found in some ways more difficult than that of Juliet. For one thing, I had to invent my own lines.

That summer I'd had a small taste of what it must mean to be a public personality. The festival was trying to recover audiences lost during the darkened war years and attract out-of-towners as well as locals: "Come Four Days, See Four Plays," the ads said, extolling the recreational opportunities in the beautiful Rogue River Valley nestled between the Cascade and Siskiyou mountains. The founder also conceived the angle of a talent-search for an actress close to the age of the real Juliet; and when I, who'd trained at the Portland Civic Theater, was awarded the role, my picture appeared in newspapers from Seattle to San Francisco.

In my mother's faithfully-kept scrapbook of that summer there's a yellowing picture of me stepping off an airplane in my Sunday-go-to-church outfit that included a navy hat with streamers, white gloves and a pair of eighteen-dollar red snake-skin heels I'd fineagled my mother into letting me buy and which I was fated not to return home with.

The newsphoto shows me squinting into the sun, juggling a copy of Stanislavsky's *An Actor Prepares* and a tennis racket locked in its frame in order to free a hand to shake that of the Founder-Managing Director. Father had fussed about the plane fare, but looking at the photo, anyone plainly can see my entrance wouldn't have had the same cachet if I'd been disembarking from a Greyhound bus.

The clippings mark the summer's progress as my short hair grows out, my sunburned nose peels, then tans, I learn to smile into the sun without squinting. There are pictures of me being fitted for my costume; one of me posed on a ladder in a Medford orchard plucking a pear—as if there were time for such things; a picture of me sitting on a park bench grimacing and clutching my ankle while my nurse, her head thrown back, guffaws. That one wasn't posed—we'd been rehearsing our lines when a cob swan waddled across the greensward to nip me.

The locals weren't sure they liked this invasion of their quiet town of porched houses and steepled churches by "those actor folks," as the old men who lazed on the bench in front of the firehouse called us: men with long hair and women who traipsed around town in shorts. Shortly after I arrived and was enjoying the sun's heat on my bare legs, one old fellow called out, "Young lady, you go home and git some clothes on you."

But by July the publicity about a young Juliet in their midst seemed to tickle the fancy of all but the most curmudgeonly. Elderly ladies stopped me on my way to the doughnut shop to take my hand and cluck, "Our little Juliet." At the diner with Romeo after rehearsals, high school kids brought me scraps of paper to autograph. (I wonder if they ever compared the signatures I inscribed; I was still wavering between a back or forward slant and whether to dot the i in my last name with a circle.)

I'd promised Grandma I'd never skip church; but the Episcopal services were at the far end of town and the hot walk from my dorm down Siskiyou Boulevard in my red high-heels led me to slip into the first parish I came to when my feet gave out—with thirty-two churches, one was always available at the first sign of an impending corn. The Sunday after I limped into the Methodist church, I was told, the pastor mentioned in his sermon young Juliet's admirably ecumenical devotion to Christ's message.

Among my bohemian family of fellow actors, I also received the attention and praise that as an only child I seemed to crave. The festival's policy was to use trained but not professional actors; most were college students, many in their late twenties and thirties, taking advantage of the G.I. Bill. Except

for the local schoolchildren who portrayed fairies in *A Midsummer Night's Dream,* I was the youngest member, and the
others treated me fondly, taking me along on outings to
Crater Lake and swim parties at the estates of wealthy Med-
fordites. When the founder wasn't looking, they'd let me take
sips of their beer. He, a kindly-uncle type, was harried and
overworked by his duties of managing the festival, directing
one of the plays and performing two major roles. He'd promised my parents "a wholesome atmosphere" and had arranged
for me to stay in the dorm where I think he hoped the middle-
aged teachers there for summer courses would keep an eye on
me.

I, of course, considered myself entirely grown-up, especially
when the older actors complimented me on my "remarkable
maturity," my "amazing poise." I also considered myself
pretty sophisticated. When one blue-eyed actor told me he'd
like to wrap me up in a candy-box and take me home to his
mother, I laughed knowingly, understanding that he and his
male roommate were lovers and the compliment contained a
deeper level of irony.

Kevin Conway, a sophomore from Stanford with carrot-red
hair and pink protruding ears who always seemed to be dog-
ging my heels, took it upon himself to warn me about the
distinguished professor of Elizabethan Studies who was to
play my nurse. Miss Halliday (as I'll call her here), didn't like
young women—"especially pretty ones," Kevin said darkly;
and recited tales of co-eds fleeing classes in tears after tongue-
lashings about sloppy scholarship. When, as befitting her
importance, Miss Halliday arrived a week late for rehearsals, I
was terrified. Never had I seen a more imposing figure. In her
floor-length, black military cape that set off the amazingly
white hair she pulled back in a severe bun, her chin held high
as Il Duce's, she didn't simply stride across the stage, she
advanced, as if there were tank treads hidden beneath the cape.
When we were introduced I must have said something that
amused her—I can't imagine what—for she threw back that

white head and laughed so heartily I saw the bottoms of her back teeth.

A few nights later I relaxed and came to love her. During rehearsal of the last scene in *Romeo and Juliet* I lay shivering on my bier in a cotton sleeveless dress as the action around me was blocked and reblocked. Right arm outstretched in command, Miss Halliday rolled out from the wings to stop the rehearsal. She swept off her cape and tucked it around me like a cozy blanket. "You fool," she scolded the startled Harvey. "Can't you see the poor child is freezing?"

All this was heady stuff. My father's side of my Portland family, a small bourgeoise army of aunts and uncles led by my widowed grandmother, never had approved of this "acting nonsense," and warned my parents that from all this attention and publicity I would get "the big head," as they put it. Out of loyalty to my mother (for it was she my father's family really disapproved of), rather than from any moral sense of proportion about not taking all this too seriously, I had resolved that I would give no appearance of being conceited or spoiled by my celebrity. This modest mien was the role I found more challenging than that of Juliet.

I know now that I'm not the only young actress who's confused her publicity with any real accomplishment. Any young creature might unwittingly charm her elders just by being fresh and possessed of a childish turn of cheek. But back then, my little secret was that I'd come to believe I was pretty special. The trick was not to let anyone know I thought so.

Backstage on opening night, I moved among my congratulators, deflecting compliments in the modest way that over the years I'd noticed that my mother made people feel good about themselves—although of course my mother meant it. *Oh, aren't you nice!... Thank you—coming from you that means a lot.... You weren't cold were you? The nights get so surprisingly chilly here....Oh my, I surely hope you had a good seat—you could hear me, couldn't you?*

A San Francisco man said I reminded him of a young Ina
Claire. I gave him a shy drop of my head: *Oh, I could never fit
in Miss Claire's shoes.* I wondered who Ina Claire was—some
has-been, I supposed.

My parents hung back, pressed against the plywood walls
of the aisle outside the dressing room, watching me with
obvious pride. I broke away from my admirers for a moment
to give my grandmother a kiss, touched that she'd taken time
off her job as a corsetiere in Lipman's bargain basement. She
was still rummaging in her handbag, perhaps for a mirror to
help her revive her feathered hat that looked like a squashed
owl after the eight-hour bus ride down from Portland.

When she finally realized that it was me pecking her cheek,
Grandma said, "Well honey, you sure seemed to know all
your words. 'Course I couldn't rightly tell. All those trucks
grinding their gears down on the highway making such a
racket."

My mother, always afraid that I'd overlook a courtesy,
urgently gestured with her thumb to someone behind me. For
a moment, I didn't recognize Billy, my high-school sweetheart
who had a summer job in Portland as a soda jerk. Still cute,
he seemed shorter than last June when I'd returned his Hi-Y
pin with promises (unkept) to write every day. I guess my eyes
had adjusted to the longer hair of the college actors; with his
sandy crew-cut and felt-and-leather jacket, Billy looked terribly
wet behind the ears.

"Billy-Billy-Billy," I said, taking his empty hands in mine.

Said Billy glumly, "I wanted to bring you roses."

Billy dug the toe of his brogan into the planks of the back-
stage floor and in a tone that suggested it was all my fault,
said, "The flower shop told me you've already got all the roses
in town. They had to close early."

Said I, "That's okay, Billy. It's the thought that counts."

Billy fiddled with the puffed shoulder of my gown. "Can't
we go someplace? I got to catch the midnight bus back. Cheez,

you know it hasn't been any fun just reading about you in the papers."

Helplessly, I waved my hands at the people milling about me and gave him a hug. He smelled of Ivory soap. It seemed a hundred years ago that I'd rested my head on his shoulder as we swayed to Claude Thornhill's "Snowfall," always the last dreamy dance of the evening.

Before the rosebuds even could open, the hot southern Oregon days wilted the bouquets that crowded the dressing room I shared with Miss Halliday and Romeo. I hauled the dead flowers to the trash bin outside the theater workshop so they wouldn't be in the way of actors using the dressing room the nights the other plays were performed.

The four plays rotated in repertory. Nights I wasn't playing Juliet, I was a curtain page, and stood straight as a sheathed dagger in tights and overblouse waiting my cue to open or close the curtains on the inner stage, a device that in the fluid Elizabethan style suggests a scene shift.

Early on, the festival founder had ruled that the plays should run, as they had in Shakespeare's time, without intermission. For a curtain page, this meant two and a half or three hours of intense listening, eyes straight ahead, seemingly oblivious to the action, to perform a small but vital role.

I may have learned as much from hanging on to every line as I did from performing myself. The gaunt actor who played King Richard II had a particularly fine voice he used to extract with enormous variety every ounce of self-pity in the tormented ego of his character. The speech Richard gives after he's deposed especially moved me when he relinquishes his worldly possessions

> and my large kingdom for a little grave,
> a little, little grave, an obscure grave. . .

Ah, how the actor lovingly stretched out that third "little" to reveal the King's false humility.

The actor who played Othello, on the other hand, began his performance with a seductively resonant timbre but by the time he was driven to kill Desdemona, he'd projected anger so long that his voice was reedy, as unconvincing as the dark greasepaint sweating off his Nordic skin.

How I wished I could have played Desdemona—loyal, sweet Desdemona, so wistfully accepting of her betrayal. When the freckled, twenty-year-old actress broke off the melody of the willow song to ask Amelia:

"Mine eyes do itch—doth that bode weeping?"

my own eyes stung. The actress was awfully good; but I thought I would have been even better. Wistfulness was my long suit.

The actress I admired the most was a tall, dark-haired beauty who portrayed Titania, Queen of the Fairies in *A Midsummer Night's Dream*. There was an air of mystery about her—although friendly enough, she didn't mix much with the rest of us—and she kept on her dark glasses even at evening rehearsals during which she kept copious notes for the directors. I fantasied that she might be having a discreet affair with one of them.

All that cool self-possession melted when Titania assumed her stage role. Standing against a pillar as curtain page, I couldn't resist watching her out of the corner of my eye as, under the trance of their misbegotten love, she garlanded the ass's head of Bottom with flowers. "Lord what fools these mortals be," crowed Puck.

Titania had such authentic poise that I wished I could have asked her how to handle Kevin Conway. If only I'd had a girlfriend, someone to giggle and let down with for a few hours, my own pose of self-possession might not have been so tiring to maintain. As the season drew toward its final days, my nerves felt raw from Kevin's braying laugh, the way he squeezed next to me in a car when we all drove over to Jacksonville or Eagle Point for dinner. At the charade parties after performance, I was always politely having to slip my shoulder from under his arm. Didn't he know I was Romeo's girl, and that he could never hope to be my type?

My mother had told me that even if I didn't like someone, "There's no excuse for not being kind." And I did feel for Kevin. With his bright red hair, oversize ears and squat, barrel-chested body, as an actor he was fated always to play clowns and fools. I wondered what it must have been like to look out at the world from those pale-lashed eyes, unable to escape from his comic body and play all the roles he surely felt within himself.

I'm sure I found Kevin irksome because I was brooding about the summer coming to an end, about not being Juliet any more and not having all the attention that came with the role. Back to our dark apartment's boredoms and the last year of high school with my hopelessly adolescent classmates I would go. Worse and more immediately bothersome, was that although my performance had received admiring reviews in the San Francisco and Portland papers, Harvey didn't seem pleased. I told myself I was being over-sensitive. How could I grow without criticism? After my next-to-last performance, the director had stormed into the dressing room and snapped, "Sweetheart. Everyone's complaining they can't hear you. You've *got to project.*"

Stung, for I thought I'd been great that night—at least I'd never *felt* the role so completely—I said defensively, "I can't help all those trucks grinding their gears down on the highway." I heard the whine in my voice. Romeo and Miss Halliday silently continued to swab greasepaint off their faces with cold cream; and I felt deeply ashamed, knowing I'd behaved unprofessionally.

The next afternoon I arrived at the theater for a run-through of *The Dream* and saw Miss Halliday on a bench deep in conversation with a plump older woman wearing a funny, feathered hat. Miss Halliday looked up and gave me a jolly wave and beckoned me over.

"Rowena," Miss Halliday said to the plump woman who

wore a navy V-necked dress that looked as if it would be hot and sticky-feeling under the bright sun, "I want you to meet our little Juliet, Mary Jane Pitts." Miss Halliday introduced the woman as Rowena Wentworth Altschull, "the critic," she added, as if of course I must know.

I told Rowena Wentworth Altschull how pleased I was to meet her and I hoped she was enjoying her stay. The woman regarded me from under her feathered hat.

Miss Halliday gave one of her famous guffaws. "Rowena, you should hear Mary Jane and the chap who plays Romeo bicker in the dressing room." (We did this because we knew it amused Miss Halliday.) "They sound like a couple forty-years married."

I grinned and said, "I guess that's how it would have been if Romeo and Juliet hadn't had all those problems with their families. If they'd lived 'happily-ever-after'."

Miss Halliday gave a wry smile and said, "Quite right, my dear, you're a wise child."

Rowena Wentworth Altschull stared at me without amusement. I blurted, "You know, you remind me an awful lot of my Grandma."

Miss Halliday hooted and Miss Altschull cooly said, "Miss Pitts, I quite assure you I have no affinities with grandmothers, yours or anyone else's," and she returned to the notebook in her lap and her conversation with Miss Halliday.

After that night's *Dream* performance, Kevin once again insisted on walking me home as he so often did on the nights that *Romeo and Juliet* didn't play and Romeo himself wasn't around to drive me back to the dorm. I protested once again that I truly liked to walk alone—the town was perfectly safe— in the starry night before I went to bed. The trouble usually was that by the time I'd finished my protestations, Kevin had followed me the whole way, about a mile and a half from the theater.

Kevin was nineteen and a drama-department student at

Stanford where I'd thought of applying—so many of the Festival actors I admired had trained there. This vagrant dream of mine (for I didn't see how my family could meet Stanford's steep tuition and I knew I didn't have the grades to earn a scholarship) gave Kevin leave to be my gratuitous mentor. "Well when you get to Stanford," he'd say; and then would follow warnings about the peccadillos of the various professors in the English and Drama departments, who was a "lech," who was an easy grader, how most girls bright enough to enter Stanford, with its restrictive legacy from Mrs. Stanford against women candidates, were "pigs." On and on, until he'd managed to rub almost all the glamour from my dream of the tile-roofed institution that simmered under the California sun waiting for me.

This night I particularly couldn't stand him. As we walked past the darkened houses, he was going on about Rowena Wentworth Altschull, bumping me with his shoulder into parking strips, and then when I switched places on the sidewalk, into the damp lawns. "Everyone's in terror about her critique of this season," Kevin said. "It's been pretty uneven, you know." Under the streetlamp I saw Kevin move his tongue arrogantly under his lower lip in a way that utterly repulsed me.

Absently, I said, "Why do we need her to critique us? The newspaper reviews were all just splendid." I particularly doted on the article in *The San Francisco Chronicle* which called me "a fetching and touching Juliet."

Kevin brayed. "Newspaper reviews! Doncha know the difference between a reviewer and a critic?"

"No, pray tell me," I said, with all the sarcasm I could marshall. I was aware of my ignorance. I couldn't follow half the references in the charades games—what was "Nude Descending Staircase with Pineapple?" Who was Penelope and why did she weave?

Kevin said, "When you get to Stanford, you'll realize that Halliday is one of the best literary critics in the country. And when you stop and think that the drama critic she respects the most is old Altschull, it'll give you some idea...." Kevin shouldered me into a patch of scratchy ivy.

I bent to pull a twig out of my sandal. "Shut up, Kevin," I muttered. "I'm not going to Stanford if you'll be there."

When I looked up I saw his pink ears turning scarlet. "Well aren't we Miss Important all of a sudden."

A terrible brattiness was welling in my chest, a true instinct no doubt dying to escape after a summer of pretending to be poised, mature and modest. "I can't stand you hanging around me all the time," I told Kevin. "Why don't you leave me alone to figure some things out for myself?"

"Hey-hey-hey," Kevin said, as if he were chiding a cat for arching its back. "You can't blame a guy for getting kind of fond."

"Oh yes, I can." I kicked him as hard as I could in the shins.

The afternoon of the final performance of the season, as I walked past the firehouse in shorts on my way to the theater, from his bench a leathery geezer grinned and tipped an imaginary hat. I waved and stopped to take a last drink from the fountain in the plaza. Over the summer I'd acquired a taste for the noxious-smelling Lithia water that came from underground mineral springs and credited my own excellent health the past months to its beneficial properties. It tasted a little like Alka Seltzer and was a particularly good antidote to an overdose of root beer and sugar doughnuts.

On my way up the steps to the theater, I tried to memorize the way the firs braided shadows and sunlight on the hillside and the image of the swans gliding so serenely on the little lake—from that distance I couldn't pick out the one that had taken such a dislike to me. On the lawn outside the chautauqua wall, actors in tee shirts and tights practiced fencing moves with wooden swords; only one performance to go and they were still working to improve it.

Another group of actors was gathered around the theater bulletin board studying long typed sheets. I saw Kevin wheel away from the board with an angry shrug. He'd kept his distance from me since that night I'd left him under a street light on Siskiyou Boulevard hopping on one foot and rubbing his damaged shin but now I was directly in his path.

"Read all about it," he said sardonically. "You can't tell the actors without a program." I asked him what was going on. "Altschull's critique," he said. *"The bitch.* She doesn't even mention me."

I waited until the others had drifted away and casually began to scan the posted broadsides. Kevin was right: I hadn't appreciated the difference between a reviewer and a critic. Much of Miss Altschull's commentary, sprinkled with phrases like *"obiter dicta,"* "moral purgation," "prodigality of imagery," went over my head. But I felt a sly pleasure at what she'd written of the actor who played Othello:

> ...instead of smouldering coals of jealousy igniting into inevitable rage, his anger peaks too early, taxing his vocal range....

Why that's just what I'd thought!

Miss Altschull heaped praise upon the freckled actress who played Desdemona. She concluded, "What a Juliet she would have made." Oh-oh, I thought. I peered over my shoulder to see if anyone were watching. On the lawn, the fencers parried, and lunged; clack-clack went their wooden swords. I skimmed the pages to the *Romeo and Juliet* review.

Of Romeo, she wrote, "he beautifully makes the transition from swaggering streetfighter to a soul enlarged by love and his tragic destiny.

"Unfortunately, little Pitts is pathetically over her head as Juliet."

That was all. I read on but the words blurred and my one-sentence dismissal rang in my ears like a maddeningly incomplete bar of music, the inner rhyme of the *ih* sounds mockingly repeating: little Pitts, path-et-ic—oh, ick, ick, ick.

The gassy Lithia water repeated in my windpipe and my mind replayed the summer with me not as Juliet the sun but as a little fool.

I could feel the flush rising on my neck as I turned away to do my part as curtain page in the afternoon run-through. Whatever you do, don't cry, I told myself. Tears would not only be unprofessional, I knew that when I did allow myself to cry, I might not stop for days.

That night after the final performance there was a cast party downtown at the barny Elks Club. The actors were relaxed and a little high, not just on the hard liquor being served but with the fondness of farewells and jokes about funny things that had happened. Everyone was as nice to me as ever and no one mentioned Miss Altschull's critique. The founder gave my hair an affectionate pull and said, "I remember your entrance from a Portland plane, clutching Stanislavski and a tennis racket. I wonder if you found use for either during the summer."

I shook my head. "You must have thought me pretty green. 'My salad days, when I was young and green,' " I quoted from *Anthony and Cleopatra*, one of the next season's productions. "I don't suppose I could come back next summer?"

He told me that he didn't know what there was for me in the line-up, but, "Sure, come to tryouts next June and we'll see."

Kevin had been standing nearby listening, and after the founder turned away, he brayed. "I suppose you thought he was going to offer you Cleopatra."

"I won't always be an ingenue," I snapped.

"Oh yes, you will," he teased. "Even when you're an old lady."

I'd liked to have kicked him again. "I suppose you think you're ever going to get to play Hamlet or Lear?" I walked away and looked around for Romeo, intending to tell him that if he wanted to leave early to drive me back to the dorm, it was okay with me. I'd say that I had to be up early to catch the

Greyhound back to Portland. What I'd mean is that we'd better allow some time for tender farewells in the front seat of his Nash.

I found him at a table with a highball in one hand and his other arm around Titania. She had her dark glasses perched on top of her lovely head and the two were talking intently. To catch Romeo's attention, I took his glass from his hand and said, "Sip?" He nodded without looking up and whispered something into the hollow of Titania's neck. I took a long drink from Romeo's glass—it must have been straight bourbon—and sputtered.

Romeo looked up and gave me a pinch on the cheek. "Hey kid, if I don't see you again, it's been great working with you," and he turned back to Titania.

I took another swig of Romeo's bourbon. "Parting is such sweet sorrow," I muttered under my breath. It suddenly came to me with sickening certainty that the reason Romeo always ended our little kiss-fests by midnight was that he was on his way to Titania's apartment. I realized with embarassed chagrin, that he'd just been baby-sitting this little ingenue, warming up for a real woman.

On my red snakeskin heels I teetered from table to table, cadging a sip of rum here, a gulp of scotch there. At one table as I reached for someone's gin glass, a dark-eyed young man with fine clean-cut features stopped my hand and took it in his. With a smile that was at the same time both friendly and grave, he said, "I saw your Juliet the other night. How lovely you were. And are."

"Well aren't you nishe to say so," I said.

Blearily, I whispered to one of the stage hands, "Who's that?"

The fellow gave me a sip of his drink and said, "He's a Medford guy home from college for the summer. War hero, I understand—friend of Romeo's from high school days. Nice guy—name's Jack Moffat."

Sunlight streaming through my dorm windows wakened

me. My mouth tasted like moldy cheese and I had no idea how I'd gotten home to bed. When I raised up to look at the clock, a force that felt like a fist smote my forehead. I fell back on the pillow. Someone rapped sharply on the door.

"Go away," I groaned. "I've died and gone to hell."

Kevin bustled into the room. "C'mon. You've got to get packed. Your bus leaves in half an hour."

As he threw my scattered clothes and books into a suitcase and cleared the closet of my tennis racket and Tchaikovsky records, I weakly asked him how I'd gotten home. "Did I do anything terrible?"

"No," he said, throwing my makeup into a paper bag. "You sorta reminded me of Ophelia's mad scene—you just wandered around in your stocking feet, vaguely singing 'The Willow Song' and 'Greensleeves' to yourself.

"After almost everyone had left, you got up and did the banishment scene from *Richard II*. Right in the middle of a line, you just keeled over." Kevin brayed. "Actually, you were pretty good. Too bad you'll never get to play Richard."

"Touché," I said, and helped Kevin pack. I still had on the cotton dress I'd worn to the party, which, although wrinkled, would do for the bus ride home. My $18.00 red snakeskin shoes were missing, probably still under a table at the Elks Club. Mother would kill me.

Kevin said he'd borrowed a car from one of the stagehands and driven me to the dorm. "But the outside door was locked, so I climbed up the drainpipe and got in the old window here and then went down and released the bolt and steered you up to bed."

"Oh lordy, did anyone see us?"

"One of the teachers was going down the hall on her way to the bathroom and put her hands over her mouth and eyes— 'see no evil, tell no evil'."

"Bless her," I said, thinking how disappointed the founder and my parents would be in me if they knew. This was real life: neither tragic or romantic but full of tedious surprises.

Not Romeo climbing a garden wall but jug-eared Kevin Conway risking his neck on a drainpipe. And the heroine with a hangover.

The bus driver started the motor when Kevin stowed my tennis racket and records on the rack above an empty seat next to a sleeping sailor. I was awfully afraid I owed Kevin at least a kiss—he stood above my seat looking ready for one.

"C'mon, move it, buddy," the driver said over his shoulder and Kevin shrugged and backed down the aisle. "Thanks," I called as he got off. "You're a real hero." I wasn't sure he heard me. He stood on the curb waving as the bus pulled out.

The sailor woke up and blinked. I waved a wan good-bye to Kevin, to the plaza and the pretty park and theater on the hill.

"Boyfriend?" the sailor asked, handing me a stick of gum.

"Are you kidding?" I said.

"What goes on in this town?" he asked, peering out the window.

"Nothin'," I said, dropping the "g" and snapping my gum like a country girl. "Nothin' goes on in this town—it's got thirty-two churches and two bars and a natural spring drinkin' fountain. Nothin' goes on in this here town."

The sailor nodded. "Bet you'll be glad to get to Portland. The big city?"

"Are you kidding?" I said and blew a gum-bubble with my tongue. The sailor went back to sleep.

When the bus made the turn on to the highway, my record album fell off the rack, the sharp corner of the cover bouncing off my aching head. I reached inside the brown cardboard liner and pulled out shellac shards of "The Moonlight Sonata." I jammed the fragments under the seat and hummed the wistful melody in my head: "Swear not, by the inconstant moon, ever changing...."

The sleeping sailor's head dropped onto my shoulder. Next summer, I decided, I would come back to the festival. I'd be a nobody. I'd eschew romance and, like a nun, live only for my vocation. I'd learn to project. I'd take the littlest, littlest role they'd give me....

I remembered King Richard's "little, *lit*-tle grave, an obscure grave" and had to laugh at myself. Medford's pear orchards blurred by and I wondered if next summer that fine-featured fellow with the grave dark eyes and friendly smile might be back in town. What was his name? Moffat? A nice name, I thought; so much more euphonious than Pitts. Gently, I eased the sailor's head off my shoulder and dozed off myself.

ROSES AND CLASS

Now that my father's gone, evenings with my mother are almost too peaceful. After dinner on a recent June visit to Portland, I poured us both a drink and, to fill the silence that in his last years Daddy so amply filled, I turned on the television.

"Oh goodie," Mother said when the picture came on the screen. "The Rose Festival princesses." She set her highball on the glass table and sat forward, her hands on her knees.

A local newscaster was interviewing a dozen pretty teenagers. The girls sat in folding chairs against a studio mural of Portland's handsome new waterfront. "*Gahd*, aren't they cute?" Mother clapped her hands. And then amended, "Course, not as cute as you were at that age."

Crossing and recrossing their legs, patting and pushing afros and flips and modified punk hairdos, giggling at the interviewer's questions ("Princess Teri, what was your most embarassing moment?"), the girls seemed caught up in some unchoreographed dance of adolescent energy. Each represented her high school in the competition for Queen of Rosaria.

"I can't believe they still do this. I thought you told me Portland had gotten so progressive." Lately, I catch myself playing my father's role, baiting her just to liven things up.

Mother poked her finger at the screen. "Why just look there. Three of the princesses are Oriental. There's even a little Negro girl."

"Black," I said. I admitted that this never could have happened in my day, which was back in the forties. "What I can't get over is how much more attractive young women are now. When's the last time you saw a truly homely teenager?"

Mother shot me a sly look. "Don't you think it's that when you yourself get older, all young people seem attractive?" She clinked the ice in her glass. "Change the channel if you want.

There's something about South American lizards on the public channel. We don't *have* to watch this if you're not interested."

"They have better cosmetics now," I said. "Eyeliners. Blushers. Blow dryers." Actually, I *was* interested. I'd never seen all the candidates for Rose Festival Queen up close. When I was in grade school they were distant dots in their formals at the civic auditorium selection of the queen and later at her coronation in Multnomah stadium. In floats high above me at the parade, they rested against pillows of flowers, waving lace-mittened hands and throwing rose petals to their subjects on the crowded sidewalks. I suspect that almost every little girl who grew up in Portland dreamed that she might one day herself be borne aloft in such blooming splendor.

On the television, Princess Bambi was telling some story about losing her little brother at the airport, her anecdote littered with "y'knows?'s" and "like's" and "he goes" as substitute for "he said."

I sighed and picked up my mother's glass to refill it. I said, "I do believe that in my day young women were a shade more articulate."

My mother said staunchly, "Not one of them is as pretty or as poised as you were at that age. You could have been Lincoln's princess—even the queen."

Around the corner in the kitchen, breaking ice out of the tray, I was startled by the vehemence in her voice. "If only you hadn't been so peculiar about that speech. To this day, I don't know what got into you. I will never, ever understand it."

What could I say? After thirty-five years, I still didn't quite understand it myself.

On a damp Monday morning in the May of 1950, I stood in the corridor outside our high school auditorium in line with a hundred and fifty other senior girls. My best friend Mona was a few girls behind me and beside me glowered the girl with whom I shared a locker. It was the first day of Rose Festival Princess Selection Week. We each were to cross the auditorium stage, give our name to the Selection Committee, smile and move on. Mr. Ford, our principal, had just told us to remember: "At Lincoln, every girl's a princess." But by this afternoon, half these princesses would be back in their class-rooms while some of us—I winked at Mona—still would be in the running.

The scent of our various colognes—Miss Dior, Tweed, Night-Scented Stock—mixed with the waft of the Spanish rice cooking in the cafeteria downstairs; and with a sour, queasy odor of excitement. I doubt that any of us had been able to eat our breakfasts.

I myself wasn't particularly nervous. For several years I'd been performing in plays at the local Civic Theater and, the previous summer, at the Shakespearean Festival in southern Oregon and had never been troubled by stage fright. I always knew my lines and today all I had to do was recite my name.

But I did wish that the moist day hadn't drooped into lank strands the pincurls I'd slept on all night. And that I hadn't chosen to wear my tailored navy crepe dress with the white collar and cuffs. By Thursday—if I survived the elimination process that long—the white trim would be filthy. Miss Har-mon had told us that morning that we were to wear the same dress each day we were in the running. "This is not a contest to see who has the best wardrobe," she said.

Miss Harmon, a crisply coiffeured woman who'd been a WAVE during the war, was the drama coach. Now she marched down the line, checking here for a crooked stocking seam, there for a shoulder bearing dandruff flakes. She stopped and told my locker-mate, Sylvia Gerber, "Tuck your buttocks under your navel, dear. You too, Mary Jane." Miss Harmon and I got on well because of my interest in the theater.

"What a farce," muttered Sylvia, the top of whose black, curly head came only to my shoulder, even in her high heels—and I was only 5'2". Sylvia didn't like her parents and this seemed to have afflicted her with a sour outlook on life; she rarely smiled and wasn't popular. I liked her though. Often she ventured cynical opinions that I'd half-way been thinking myself but wouldn't have said aloud, even if I'd been able to put them into words. Sometimes on Saturdays we went to the Guild to see foreign films oozing with existential despair—a fine way, I thought, to spend a rainy Portland afternoon.

"At least this weather doesn't take the curl out of your hair," I said to Sylvia. "No," she said acidly. "It just turns it into a brillo pad." I wondered if any girl in the school was satisfied with her hair; maybe Tessa Cohen, whose dark ringlets, rain or shine, always looked disgustingly perfect.

I was touched that even though she thought all this was a farce, Sylvia had worn a pretty dress and pearl earrings. As if she had a chance. I hoped that she'd be spared the humiliation of being eliminated the first day.

I looked down the long line of senior girls and knew which ones wouldn't be in the running tomorrow: the fat girls, the girl with one leg shorter than the other, the ones with bad acne, the girls who wore tight skirts and hung around with the Broadway Boys, a gang of rowdies. Girls who were poor and plain and didn't get into clubs, like sweet Mary Theresa Kowalski, with whom I'd been friends in grade school but now only waved to in the halls.

Not all the Japanese, Chinese and Negro girls would be bumped today. After all, the theme of this spring's yearbook was "One World." As Portland's only west side high school, Lincoln had a cosmopolitan student body, drawing, as the yearbook said, "people from all races and religions, and from all walks of life who study and associate happily together." Still, there were unwritten distinctions.

I remember once when I was seven or eight and my one uncle who owned a car drove a visiting relative, along with my parents and me, on a tour of the city. When we entered Portland Heights with its gabled houses and lovely gardens, I said to our visitor, "This is where the upper classes live." When we were alone, my mother chided me. "In America there is no upper class. We're all the same." "Then how come..." I asked her why my Chinese friends had to live in storefronts down by the train station. How come even if she and my father worked hard we lived in an old apartment house in a crummy neighborhood. "That's just the way it is," Mother said.

And now I ran around with the kids who lived on the Heights or in Dunthorpe or out at the lake; I belonged to almost all the right clubs at school and the best all-city sorority. I'd made it. And Sylvia, who lived in the right part of town and whose parents owned a house at Seaside, hadn't. And by Friday when six senior girls gave their speeches to the student body so one could be chosen to represent our school as Rose Festival Princess, the six would be popular, pretty and white. That's just the way it is, I thought.

The line moved forward and it was Sylvia's turn to cross the auditorium stage, then it would be mine. I tucked my buttocks under my navel and whispered to Sylvia, "Good luck."

"This whole thing is barbaric," Sylvia said.

That evening while Mother fixed dinner and I sat on the sofa reading the funnies, my father looked up from his book and said, "Your mother tells me you passed the first day of Rose Princess week."

"Yeah," I said, deep in Gasoline Alley.

"*Yah*? What are you? German?"

"Yes," I corrected myself.

"Well, you don't act very thrilled."

"It's no big deal," I said. "Passing the first day." I put down the newspaper. "Sylvia didn't, though. Pass."

"Sylvia's practically a midget. I don't believe I've ever seen a midget Rose Festival princess."

"It's not funny," I said. "The whole thing doesn't seem very fair."

"Fair? Where is it written that life is fair? If life were fair, do

you think your mother would be working her heart out down
at that office? She's smarter than any of her bosses. If life were
fair, your mother would own that company."

"Oh come on. You know what I mean."

Daddy looked over his glasses at me. "I hope you're not
going to wear that plain-Jane dress again tomorrow. You
look like a prison matron in that dress. What about that pink
one your mother got you?"

"Have to," I said. "The rules." I giggled. "Mona told me
Tessa Cohen was furious. Her mother's a seamstress and made
her five different gorgeous dresses to wear this week."

"Tessa who?" My father put his finger in his book to keep
his place and closed it.

"Tessa Cohen."

"She can't be very smart if she thinks she stands a chance
with a name like Cohen."

"Sure she does," I said. "Our school is very democratic.
Tessa and her family escaped from Germany. If she won, it'd
fit into our 'One World' theme perfectly."

"You like her?" my father asked.

I shrugged. Wasn't it true that I was a bit jealous of Tessa? I
asked myself. Not of her extraordinary dark beauty, although
she made the rest of us in our crowd of girlfriends look like
pale daisies alongside a crimson rose. But of the fact that she
lived in a run-down house in the wrong part of town and, like
me, had still made it with the right set at school?

"Well I'll tell you frankly," I said. "I was shocked when I
heard today that she's had her speech written for a whole
year."

"What speech?"

I told him about the speech the six finalists had to give on
Friday before the student body. "I mean, don't you think
that's kind of arrogant? To write your speech even before you
know you'll be a finalist?"

"No," my father said. "It sounds like she knows how to
work hard for what she wants. Everything's always come so

easily to you." Father was still a little miffed that Mother had said she'd find a way to pay for my tuition at Stanford where I'd been accepted for next fall. He didn't see why I couldn't go to the less expensive University of Oregon. Or stay home and work for a year and save.

"Have you thought about your speech?" he asked.

"Of course not," I said. "I don't even know if I'm going to make the final six."

"Well even so, maybe it wouldn't hurt to start thinking about one," Father said.

On Tuesday afternoon Mona and I found our names on the list of sixty remaining candidates. I gave Mona's hand a little squeeze and she squeezed back. It would have hurt both of us if one were dropped before the other. Today there were no more Oriental names on the list—no Negro girls had survived the first day. Tessa, of course, was still in the running. I wondered, since she'd had her speech and gowns prepared in advance, what other campaign efforts she was making. I was beginning to realize it *was* a campaign, not just an honor a girl passively waited to have bestowed upon her.

Mona was a tall, round-faced blonde of Dutch ancestry whose sister had been Rose Princess a few years ago. She was deservedly well-liked, a sunny, kind and bright girl, and I thought she stood a good chance of becoming a finalist, even princess. I asked her if she'd given any thought to a speech, "just in case."

"Of course I don't expect to make it," she said in her high, pure voice. "But sure, I've thought about it. Haven't you?"

I groaned and told Mona there were basically only two formulas I'd heard in Rose Princess speeches and I couldn't stand either one. "There's 'The Beauty of the Rose' number," I said, "that starts out with the little sprout pushing its way up through the hard soil, sending down deep roots and getting kissed by the sun and blessed by the rain until one day to bring beauty to the world it unfurls its splendor, a teardrop of dew on its velvet petal.

"Then there's the fairy tale that always starts out with a sad princess and ends with a prince breaking her spell with a perfect rosebud that has a teardrop of dew on its velvet petal."

Mona flushed and I saw that she'd more than thought about her speech. I'd probably just quoted one of its lines.

On Wednesday night when I told my mother that Mona and I had made the list of thirty remaining girls, she said, "Your father said something about a speech. Don't you think you'd better start writing one?"

"I think that's cheating," I said. "I'll write one when and if I'm chosen."

"But that could be tomorrow night," Mother said. "And then you'd have to memorize it. I don't understand you. Don't you want to be Rose Festival Princess?"

"Of course, I do," I snapped. Who wouldn't want to be Rose Festival Princess? Riding high above the crowd on a pillow of flowers, waving to her subjects. Maybe even getting to be the queen who wore a crown and an ermine robe. Didn't every girl who grew up in Portland dream of that? And here I was, one of the lucky few who'd even come close to having the chance. But something within me would not let me think about that speech until and unless it was absolutely necessary.

By Thursday it was absolutely necessary. After school I was at the library looking up "Rose" in the card catalogue. Tessa, Mona and I, along with Francine Rodeway—a voluptuous girl from the Northwest side—and two girls from the Heights, had been selected to be the final six to compete in tomorrow's ten o'clock assembly.

I was in an absolute panic. "Roses: *cultivation of*." "Roses: *diseases of*." "Roses: *War of the*." Over the years hundreds of princess candidates must have been in my pickle—wouldn't you think the card catalogue would list, "Roses: *sappy speeches about*"?

At home that evening as I sat in my room facing a blank piece of paper, I heard my parents tiptoeing about. My mother spoke in urgent, low tones. My father's voice was perfectly audible. "If every other girl with any intelligence wrote out a speech in advance and only six were chosen, why doesn't she just call up one of the girls who didn't make it and borrow her speech?"

I heard my mother mutter something admonitory. My father said, "Well it seems dumb to let all those perfectly good speeches go to waste. Especially since she can't seem to think one up."

I chewed my pencil. It was getting late. Pretty soon I'd have to take my bath and set my hair in pincurls. Why was I having so much trouble? I easily turned out slick essays for my English classes.

In the airshaft outside my bedroom window, the pigeons were cooing their goodnights. Suddenly a truth descended on me.

I hated roses.

I thought of the thorny bushes in their regimented rows in the International Test Garden at Washington Park, each bearing a clamped metal label: Henry Ford; Mrs. Miniver; Crimson Glory. In the winter when the gardeners pruned them back to their bare bones, the bushes were fiercely ugly. When summer came and the plants presented their heavily scented blooms, the gardeners kept at them, dusting their yellowing leaves for black spot, spraying for cankers that can blight the buds before they open. In a vase, the stiffly formal perfect rose so quickly turned blowsy, and then shed its petals like a slattern strewing her clothes.

I loved field flowers: daisies and cornflowers, violets and Queen Anne's Lace. Trilliums that sprouted on creek banks with no ambition to be admired; blooms that just came into the world on their own, without grooming or tending.

But this insight was of no use in helping me write a speech about the rose. The page before me still was blank. At eleven, I soaked in the tub and tried to think of an opening sentence while I shaved my legs. A knock on the door told me it was my father—Mother would have just barged right in.

"What?" I said.

Father opened the door a crack and put his hand over his eyes to show he wasn't looking at my nakedness. "Honey, I just had an idea."

"Shoot," I said. I was desperate.

"I know you don't want to want to give a mushy speech about the rose." I'd told him about the usual formulas and that I thought they were sickening.

"You could stress the commercial angle," he said.

"What commercial angle?"

"Rosaria's an invention of the Chamber of Commerce—a way to get tourists into town and everybody to spend a lot of money."

"It is?" This had never occurred to me and I wished he hadn't pointed it out. All that magic, ever since I was a little girl—I couldn't stand to think of a lot of bald-headed business men producing it.

"I was thinking maybe you could do a comparison study of festivals and pageants. The Mummer's Parade in Philadelphia, Mardis Gras in New Orleans. You could talk about how a festival fills up hotel rooms, how the restaurants would go broke without one—of course, it would take some research and it's getting pretty late...."

I sighed. "Thanks, Daddy. It's certainly not mushy. But somehow I don't think it would be a crowd-pleaser." If I focused on full hotel rooms and restaurants, how would I work in the teardrop of dew on the rose's velvet petal? "Don't worry, Daddy, something will come to me."

Father shut the bathroom door. As soon as I'd said, "Something will come to me," I began to relax. Father said things came to me easily. Why not a speech? I knew an appropriate one must be stored someplace in my brain. I never got stage fright; I always knew my lines. These lines I just hadn't quite found yet because I'd been looking too hard. Tomorrow I'd see the audience out there and my old stage presence would take over. I'd just open my mouth and a speech would come out.

I could almost see a large cartoon balloon containing a perfect speech floating above the stage.

When I arrived at school the next morning, Sylvia was at our locker. I squashed my raincoat into my messy side.

"God, you must be sick of that dress," Sylvia said.

I was. Even though Mother had laundered the collar and cuffs and tacked them back on, the armholes felt rancid. The backs of my thighs were chafed from the metal fasteners of the garter belt I'd had to wear all week. Sylvia looked so comfortable in her Peter Pan blouse, Sloppy Joe sweater and saddles with bobby sox.

"What are you going to say in assembly?" Sylvia asked.

My brain felt detached from my body, hovering someplace off to the left. "You'll see," I said. I was mildly curious myself. "It's sort of a surprise."

The six princess candidates were excused from our home rooms to practice our speeches, one by one, before Miss Harmon. I asked to be last. When my turn came, I gave our drama coach my most winning smile. "I think it might spoil it if I said it ahead of time," I told her. "Sound over-rehearsed."

She cocked her head to one side. "Mary Jane, what is your speech about?"

"I don't know," I said. "I mean I know; but I don't know *yet.*"

Miss Harmon shook her head in dismay. "You, of all people," she said. "Can I help?"

"Don't worry, Miss Harmon. It will come to me."

Mr. Ford had us draw lots before he introduced us. Mona went first. Her variant on the fairy tale took the point of view of the princesses' sad, homely little sister, who hoped one day to grow up and be as beautiful, loving and kind to her subjects as Sis. It was a good angle. Who could blame a little kid for loving all this?

Tessa next told a tale of an ogre who cut off the heads of roses whose colors he didn't like. The ogre, she explained, represented the scourge of fascism. She pronounced scourge as if it rhymed with "George." After a whole year of practicing it, I thought meanly, someone might have pointed this out to her. The ogre was defeated and all the different colored roses lived happily together in the garden, teardrops of dew on their velvet petals. She got a lot of applause and I had to hand it to her. I wished I'd thought of bending the subject of roses to the One World theme.

Then Mr. Ford introduced me and I crossed the stage to stand before the microphone and smile. I made eye contact with the freshmen and sophomores in the balcony. I smiled at the teachers sitting on the left, the seniors in the middle and the juniors on the right side of the auditorium. I waited for my speech to come.

But only odd phrases reeled through my mind:

There comes a time in the course of human events . . .

In Xanadu did Kubla Khan . . .

The boy stood on the burning deck . . .

Suddenly, I was back in a deadball game in grade school, watching the ball hurl toward me and I too paralyzed either to catch it or move out of its way. There was a titter or two from the audience at this long silence. Mr. Ford cleared his throat. I stopped smiling.

"I find I have nothing to say about the rose," I said, and took my seat.

Although I kept my head down when we returned to our classes after the assembly to vote, in a way it was as if it had happened to someone else, some part of me I didn't need to claim just yet. Just before lunch, Mr. Ford announced over the loudspeaker that Tessa Cohen was Lincoln's Rose Festival Princess and that Francine Rodeway, as runner-up, would be Queen of the May.

Later in the day, Sylvia found out and told me that Mona had come in third, and I, not last as I thoroughly deserved, but fourth. It almost made me mad. Even I hadn't voted for myself but for Mona. What could those who voted for me have been thinking of? I suppose I got a few votes from kids like Sylvia who thought the whole thing a farce. And maybe Mary Theresa Kowalski, whom I'd so blithely left behind, remained proud that someone from her grade school had made it that far.

Tessa made a splendid Rose Princess. At the civic auditorium in June, she gave another effective speech in the competition between the princesses elected by the other high schools. Although she was surely the most beautiful, she wasn't chosen to be Queen of Rosaria. Father speculated that the Chamber of Commerce wasn't ready for a Queen with a Jewish name. I don't know. I do know that I felt a bit sorry for Tessa—having to dress up every day to attend charity teas and Rotary banquets while the rest of us lazed through the last sunny days of our senior year.

The morning I was to go back to San Francisco after my recent visit, my mother and I sat in the living room drinking coffee. We'd exhausted the gossip about our relatives and pretty much finished her tidbits about her neighbors, in whom I was even less interested than in cousin Francie's latest boyfriend. An exercise program was on the television but Mother had turned down the sound. She stared at the screen with the sad look she always gets when I'm going to leave.

Watching the lithe instructor bend and stretch on TV, I said, "Did I ever tell you I saw Tessa Cohen at the reunion last year?"

"No!" Mother clapped her hands and sat forward. "How'd she look?"

"Gorgeous," I said. "She's wealthily divorced. All she does is raise German Shepherds and exercise."

"Did you and she have anything to talk about?"

"I think I was a little high. I dropped by her table and told her how to pronounce 'scourge'."

"I don't get it," Mother said.

"Neither did she," I giggled. "After the class president gave the prize to the person who had the most grandchildren, I got up to the mike and made a little speech myself."

"What'd you say?"

"I said, 'Over the years, I've given the matter considerable thought; and I find I still have nothing to say about the rose.' "

"Oh lord," Mother said, shaking her head in dismay. "What was the reaction?"

"A few people smiled. I don't think very many remembered."

Mother said, "Your father always said that you deliberately sabotaged yourself by wearing that plain dress. He said he told you that you'd be sorry, but stubborn you, you wouldn't listen."

I laughed. Here he was back in the room with us again. I could almost hear his voice. I took a sip of coffee. It had grown cold. "I've never been sorry," I told them both. "I just never cared for roses."

GOODBYE, CITY OF ROSES

Letter Home

IN THE FALL OF 1951 when Korean truce talks were droning on in Panmunjon, I worried more about legally losing my virginity than distant political squabbles. From my dorm room at Stanford, where I was a sophomore drama major, I wrote my parents in Portland asking their permission to be married over the Christmas break.

"Please don't worry about this costing you a lot of money," I wrote. "Jack and I'll be happy with a simple ceremony at City Hall."

I sent the fateful letter with its six cent air mail stamp on a Tuesday morning. As soon as the mailbox slot clanked close, I wished I could call back my words.

That night I said to my intended, "They'll say no." Jack was a hard-working Graduate School of Business student seven years my senior—I was eighteen. "They'll say I'm too young. They'll worry I'll drop out of school."

We were sitting in his green Studebaker outside Branner Hall, about to use up another of my late-leaves after a prolonged session of amouressness we'd once again barely managed to stop in time.

"Tell them how much more studying we'll get done," Jack said, his voice clabbered with frustration. In those days even a sophisticated war veteran could believe in honoring his beloved by waiting. The fleshly tumult of over a year of keeping me technically chaste had just about fried our brains.

"The truth is," I sighed as I watched dorm lights blink out, "I'm not sure my parents can bear to give me up yet. You've got to realize, I'm all they have. This could break their hearts."

"Tell them how much more studying we'll get done," Jack said, buttoning up my Peter Pan blouse.

2.
Courtship and Goodness

I decided to wait until Saturday afternoon to telephone my parents for their response. Enough time for them to calm down and absorb the idea. My father would probably be out on the weekly grocery bargain-hunt he and I used to take together. Mother would be back upstairs from the basement laundry room of our apartment house and I knew I could count on her to tell me whatever they'd decided in a gentler fashion than Father.

The next two days I wandered half-conscious to my classes, knowing there was no way I could make both my parents and Jack happy in this world. It never occured to me to wonder if all this fretting might not be confusion about what would make *me* happy.

In Shakespeare class on Thursday, the professor explained that when Hamlet tells Ophelia to "get thee to a nunnery," the prince meant not a cloister but a house of harlotry. I blurted, "Oh no!" and kindly plump Dr. Whittaker peered at me over his glasses while the other students tittered. Hamlet's sarcasm had reminded me of my father's, and I could fantasy my parent saying something equally withering.

If I could pinpoint the exact moment when my girlhood—and daughterhood—began to end, it would be the summer of 1950 when I stood before the casting board at the Oregon Shakespearean Festival in Ashland. The previous year I'd starred as Juliet and all the publicity and attention had given me a pretty good case on myself. But as my eye ran down the casting sheet (I'd hoped at the very least to play Bianca in *The Taming of the Shrew*), I saw that all I'd been listed for was the small role of Phoebe, a shepherdess in *As You Like It*. For a brief moment I considered returning to Portland; until I remembered the file-clerk job that waited me there. I decided that this theatrical come-down would improve my character, like giving up chocolate for Lent.

But I groaned when I read that I'd also been assigned to assist with the lights for *Henry IV, Part I*. This was carrying humiliation too far—to ask a gifted actress to perform lowly technical work! I'd never understood the devotion of back-stage workers. Why do it, if you couldn't be out front receiving the laughter and applause?

But I cheered up at the first technical rehearsal when I discovered that I was to assist Jack Moffat, a finely knit Cal Tech graduate I'd caught a glimpse of the summer before. "I guess I lucked out," he grinned, giving me a comradely pat on the shoulder as he showed me the switchboard. "Just don't try and explain electricity to me. I'm hopeless at that kind of stuff," I said.

Right away, I felt easy with him, as if he were the older brother I'd never had. He took a light pleasure in the simplest things, from opening a can of beer to noticing when I wore a new off-the-shoulder peasant blouse. I didn't associate his kind of dash with engineering types; at the same time, he seemed real—firmly himself—in a way that escaped my actor friends with their florid speech and gestures.

I was in no mood for summer romances after a disappointing one with the actor who'd played Romeo the summer before. And I had all those Stanford men—where males out-numbered females five to one—to look forward to in the fall.

Still, working in the darkened light booth under Jack's calm instructions was seductively intimate. When he whispered a cue, I'd smell the tobacco and Colgate toothpowder of his breath, the tang of fresh sweat mixed with the Palmolive he'd scrubbed with earlier.

When he'd tried to enlist in the navy in 1942, he'd tested color-blind; so our heads were often close when he had trouble telling the difference between the red and yellow switches on the Davis board. "That's right, ease her up now," he'd say in a voice slightly rasped by cigarettes, and I'd feel against my brow the feathery brush of his crewcut and the warm glance of his forearm on mine.

I pried out of him that he'd been an infantry sergeant and had been wounded in the Battle of the Bulge. "Where?" I asked, dazzled by this proximity with an authentic war hero. He gave a wry laugh. "The part of you that sticks up the farthest when you're crawling on your belly." He wouldn't add anything more about the war. "Let's just say it wasn't a hell of a lot of fun."

On afternoons off when a crowd of us swam at one of the Medford pools, I watched the way Jack dived like a missile, his arms at his side instead of over his head. I later learned his left shoulder easily dislocated; but instead of looking like a precautionary measure, the way his head broke the skin of turquoise water seemed some enviable new style. When he surfaced, he always was smiling and I came to notice that his eyes sought out mine before he kick-stroked to the ladder to dive again.

A poor swimmer myself, I usually reclined in a deck chair basting my body with baby oil—I didn't want to look like an Oregon webfoot at Stanford that fall. Baked by the dry valley heat, one day I took to the water, dog-paddling, and a firm clasp around my ankle in a rushing second pulled me to the bottom of the pool where firm lips kissed my sputtering mouth closed. Then I was propelled up again into the air, coughing, laughing, phlegm streaming from my nose. I glanced around to see if anyone had witnessed this audacity but the actors and crew members were drinking colas, talking, and then Jack popped up beside me, wiped my nose with the heel of his hand and swam away. I'd always hated boyish highjinks; but this felt different: an amusing conferral of honor, an invitation into a realm I'd never before entered.

That night I stood by the lighting console watching Jack's profile as he peered through the slot at the stage action for our next cue. In the dim light, I admired the economy of his body: his straight nose, the way he held one shoulder higher than the other in expectation, the way his narrow hips tapered down into the legs of his chinos. There was nothing extra about him. His bare feet—it was hot in the booth despite the chill outside now that the sun had gone down—were firmly planted on the wood planks and he seemed like some kind of rod, a conduit of certainty.

Near the end of the third act, as the king chastised Prince Hal for his wastrel ways, utterly without volition I put my arms around Jack's shoulders and let my head rest against the back of his neck. I sensed a click of pause in his muscles and then he turned and embraced me with a kiss so long and deep that, in a swoon, I stumbled backward and sat down on the Davis board, completely blacking out Act III, Scene 3 of *Henry IV, Part I.*

On the stage, bathed in ghostly moonlight, King Henry ad-libbed, "A light, prithee, send forth a light!" It took Jack and me two fumbling minutes to restore the illusion of a fifteenth century English morning.

At the post-performance critique, the director ground his teeth when he came to the matter of the third act blackout. How in God's name had it happened? Head down, I said lamely, "It was entirely my fault." No, Jack insisted, it was entirely *his* fault; and then we looked at each other and broke out laughing. The glowering director was not amused. For my part, I couldn't stop whooping at the thought that in one day I'd received the two most dramatic kisses of my lifetime: one stolen underwater and the second casting five hundred people into darkness.

Later that night as we cuddled in his car, Jack put on a serious look belied by the laughter in his eyes and said, "After a disgrace like that, I guess we have to get married."

Alarmed by new feelings strumming in my nethers, I pushed him away. "Don't tease. Is this just a summer romance?" If so, I told him, I thought we'd better stop right now. I sensed that I wouldn't get over this one easily, if ever.

Jack got out of the car and opened the door on my side. He

led me by the hand to stand on the hillside where we'd parked. Beneath the star-pricked sky, immense and silent, families slept safely in the darkened houses; only a few lonely-looking headbeams defined the highway.

Jack said I'd been on his mind since the summer before. His words came out awkwardly, as if they cost him a lot. "You're the kind of girl that when I'd see some guy out with her, I'd think, *that lucky bastard.*"

He smoothed down my hair and said that he too was afraid of his feelings. The idea that had been forming in his mind the past weeks that we might marry and spend the rest of our lives together had given him, for the first time since he'd returned from the war, some hope that the world might have a future.

"Before you," he said, "I wouldn't let myself count on anything. I had a good time at Cal Tech, made some neat friends, had a lot of laughs. But all the time I wondered why I was studying when the world is just going to blow up anyway."

We sat on the gravelly berm and let our legs dangle in the dried grasses of the hillside. I knew that something called a Cold War was going on but it never struck me that it had much to do with me. Jack spoke of an atomic clock inching toward midnight and shook his head. "It doesn't seem right to bring children into such a mess."

"Why, everyone wants children," I said hotly. I'd never actually thought out the concept of my own, or how their arrival would fit into the career of a famous actress. Having children someday was just one of those givens in life. Hadn't my mother told me often that I was the one great thing that had happened to her?

"You've got to have faith," I told Jack, feeling a little odd in advising this older man who knew so much.

He told me that his parents were devoted Episcopalians but that after the age of eight he'd flatly refused to go to church. "I just decided the whole thing was a shuck."

I was aghast. I'd bring him back into the fold, I thought, not the first lass to begin plotting reforms in her newly beloved.

An invisible owl uttered its questioning calls and furtive scurryings in the weeds made me tuck my bare legs under my dirndl as I discovered there were a few other matters to be negotiated. Jack was a Republican. I couldn't vote for four years yet but I'd idolized Franklin Roosevelt and won a five dollar bet from my grandmother when Truman trounced Dewey. I liked traditional furniture, the good stuff my parents had cheap versions of. I described my ideal gabled house and Jack groaned: "It sounds like my folks' place.

"I shouldn't tell you this, but I've already sketched a floor plan for us. The kitchen is in the middle—open to the living room. You'll never have to feel shut away."

"I can't cook," I confessed.

"That's okay," he said cheerfully. "I can. While I make dinner, you can read me plays. Do you like Sartre?"

I'd never heard of Sartre; or, as Jack told me more about his enthusiasms, of Kandinsky or Klee or Erik Satie. He seemed so all of a piece, while I felt like a collection of loose parts and ideas rattling around in a drawer.

"You'll have to wait for me to finish college," I said, "for me to catch up with you." To grow up, I thought, wondering if he would wait that long or if a real woman wouldn't snatch him away before I could learn enough to hold up my end of the conversation. "I bet there's a lot of things you'd like to change about me."

"Nothing," he said. "You're all the parts of me that are missing. You're my ego now."

We opened our eyes from a kiss to a watercolor sunrise of pink cherubic clouds. In my apartment-house past, I'd witnessed few dawns. In some ways, this new morning was the moment in my life when I felt most truly married.

The following year at Stanford was harder, truer. Along with four other grad students, Jack rented a ramshackle cabin in the hills behind the university where he spent long hours studying. How serious he'd become now that the prospect of supporting me had given him belief in a future.

At my dorm room desk, I sat trying to learn how to study but too often bleakly staring out at the brown hills. The impetuous summer of swimming parties and greeting the dawn seemed long ago in another emotional country, replaced by the burned-spice smell of eucalyptus which as the months wore on I came to associate with loneliness.

Never afflicted by homesickness as a girl, now I'd come down with a bad case. Not for my parents or for Portland—I was happy to have them just where they were, on the borders of my consciousness.

I didn't fit into the girlish world of my dorm-mates who went off to mixers and dances, who fretted about dates for the Big Game or plotted retaliation for the latest panty raid. But when Jack emerged from his books, as a minor, I couldn't go to bars with him and his friends. Nor did I have anything to say to his housemates' girlfriends who were getting their teaching credentials and chatted about silver patterns and ideal family size (six kids to fill a wood-panelled station wagon with an Irish setter panting out the window).

I was homesick for a place that didn't exist yet, a steady life with Jack who was fast becoming full family to me: parent, brother, best friend as well as one day lover-husband. Yet this advance nostalgia for a home together had a curious vagueness. In my mind, all I saw was a double bed in a room with a door that locked.

Jack talked me into taking a two-unit elective called "The Modern House" but I just couldn't get interested in what the textbook called "A machine for living" with its stark Eames chairs and bunk beds for the children. By now, Jack wanted "a houseful," he said, a thought that somehow made me glum. It was May; Truman had just recalled MacArthur from Korea; Senator McCarthy was finding Communists under cabbage leaves. With mordant brightness, I asked Jack, "What about the atomic clock? Do you really think it's fair to plan on children in such a world?"

"We've got to have faith," Jack said, popping a Tums under his tongue. He'd taken on two part-time jobs in addition to his studies and had developed a nervous stomach.

In the way a bored child wishes something exciting to happen—a plane falling from the sky onto her familiar neighborhood—I half-hoped for some cataclysmic event beyond my control to alter my direction. Jack didn't even want to take time off for a swim in Lake Lagunita. We always had to get to where we were going. And where we were headed would turn out to be that long grey tunnel of so-called fifties normalcy.

If there was a way around the tunnel, I didn't have the heart, courage or wits to explore it. Cast as Portia's lady-in-waiting in the drama department production of *Merchant of Venice*, I met a famous old character actor who'd come out from New York to play Shylock. After rehearsal one night, this bulbous-nosed man took me aside and showed me how to put some style in my bland role.

"You've got something, kiddo," he told me. "Why don't you come to New York. I'd be glad to help you get some auditions."

I gasped. "New York?"

"That's where ambitious actors usually begin," he said drily. "Unless you plan to waste away out here in the provinces."

"But I have to..." What was it I had to do?

He gave an elaborate sigh and finished my sentence. "Have to marry that ordinary young man who waits so patiently for you every night? Have to bear a slew of children?" He waved his hands in dismissal. "I shouldn't have wasted my breath. I didn't realize you were so middle-class."

"He is not ordinary," I muttered, and left the great actor to his mellifluous brooding and strode out to meet my beloved. It did strike me as comic that my parents were going broke sending me to school so I could break into the middle-class. And now before I even got there, the old crock was advising me to break out of it.

I had to go back to Portland that summer and work as a file-clerk in an insurance company. I pined for Jack who'd gotten a laborer's job at a steel mill in southern California. Never had my hometown seemed so ordinary and when I returned from work, the smell of stale cigar smoke and cabbage dinners in our apartment house corridors—the odor of disappointment and failure—turned my stomach. I couldn't wait to get out of there.

Father took some malicious pleasure at my complaints about the numbing boredom of filing insurance claims. "Now you know what it means to work for a living. Ha! And it isn't even a living."

Mother, when she wasn't at the dining table shuffling bills and wondering where she was going to borrow money for tuition for my sophomore year (I hadn't earned good enough grades for a scholarship), worried more about the letters that arrived every day in our garbage chute in creamy Crane envelopes from Jack. "It occurs to me," she said one Saturday morning, "that I've neglected to teach you how to wash clothes"; and she dragged me down to the basement laundry room with its wringer machines and pull-out racks for drying.

I'm afraid I wasn't a very good student. When she explained the importance of bluing and starch, I said, "Nobody bothers with that stuff anymore. In my dorm, you just toss the clothes into the Bendix washer and dryer and that's that."

"I saw your clothes when you got home. I was mortified. You didn't even separate the whites from the coloreds. Worse than Midge. (My alcoholic uncle's wife who occupied the lowest station in the in-law pecking order.) And where is it written that you will have an automatic washing machine in your future life?"

"Don't you remember?" I asked sassily. "I'm going to be a rich and famous actress and put you and Daddy up in a mansion. We'll have a Bendix in every room."

Down there in the dark laundry room with lace curtains stretched on frames with pins and other tenants' pajamas and sheets encroaching on the pull-out dryer Mother long ago had staked out as her own, our old game of all I was going to do for them when I was rich didn't seem so bonny anymore. Our eyes met as I handed her clothespins for my father's socks. Strands of mousey-brown hair fell across her brow, shiny from the steam. "Your grandmother was right," she said sadly. "I gave you all the wrong kinds of lessons. I must have been dreaming."

In late August, Jack wrote that he was driving to Portland for the Labor Day weekend with an engagement ring he'd had a modernist jewelry maker design. Mother fretted about this visit. "Why with all his degrees, I won't know what to say to him." She wanted to Kem-Tone the living room walls.

"He'll just have to take us as we are," Father said. But I noticed that on the Saturday morning before Jack arrived, he applied Old English to the furniture until the nicks and cigarette burns gleamed. He kept standing back from his flower arrangements with a critical eye, changing the nod of a rose here, the droop of a fern there, while my mother shrieked for help in the kitchen where one of her jars of home-preserved tomatoes had just exploded into great dauby splats on the already mottled ceiling.

If they were nervous, I was paralyzed. I hadn't told them about the ring. After our laundry room lesson, Mother had told me to wash my own clothes. I had nothing clean to wear and now it was getting too late for a shampoo—Father had commandeered the bathroom. I got myself up in one of his frayed dress shirts that I let hang over a New-Look (old by then) black skirt that trailed to my ankles. I put on flat ballet practice shoes so Jack would look taller beside me and when I skinned back my limp hair into a pony tail and looked in the mirror, I decided I looked like a struggling Greenwich Village actress. At least not middle-class.

When Jack arrived he gave me a long kiss, right in front of my parents; when it was over, Father was rearranging a bouquet and Mother was regarding the ceiling. Jack took in the apartment in a quick, mildly surprised glance. I *had* misrepresented things a bit, I realized, as when I'd alluded to Father's collection of Oriental art, which was just a four-inch brass buddha on a teakwood stand and a set of plaster figurines he'd once bought in San Francisco's Chinatown.

I'd misrepresented Jack a bit to my parents as well. That evening as he and my mother led the way up the stairs to a Chinese restaurant, my father, vain of his own height, whispered, "He's not very tall." "Neither am I," I snapped. "We fit together very well." "Izzat so?" my father said with one of his arched-brow looks.

Later, in the ladies room, Mother said, "Why he's so easy to talk to—and he has such lovely manners. And on him, a crew cut isn't too bad." I knew she was thinking of Father's thick head of dark curly hair with its part so straight it looked as if he used a ruler.

Back at the apartment, the two men sat up late playing Dixieland albums Jack had brought from his vast collection, Father in sickening ecstacy over Kid Ory and the Firehouse Five, Jack slapping his thigh to the beat, his brown eyes dancing with more happiness than I'd seen in a long time. He'd seemed to lose his capacity for fun this past year, always talking about our dream house, how much money he'd need to earn for us to be "comfortable." ($10,000 a year, he figured, would do it.)

Not having seen Jack all summer, I'd imagined that we might take a drive somewhere by ourselves, but by midnight, when they were deep into Bessie Smith, I gave up and said goodnight. I felt something sour in my stomach that felt like jealousy and for the first time I wondered what it would have been like for my father to have had a son.

The three-day visit passed to everyone's delight but mine, for Jack and I never did have much time alone. He repaired a lamp my mother thought she'd have to give to the Goodwill. He and my father both had a perfect memory for jokes and their laughter filled the whole apartment while they collaborated on a spaghetti sauce over our old gas range. For propriety's sake, Jack had slept on a daybed in the apartment above ours my grandmother shared with my aunt and uncle. When it came time to say goodbye, even cool Grandma gave Jack a wet smack on the cheek. "He sure does know his way around a kitchen," she said with a dark look at me.

"I like your folks," Jack said when we were back at Stanford for fall quarter, once again wrapped around each other in the front seat of the Studebaker. "You all seem to be so open with each other. How come you didn't show them the ring?"

"They liked you too," I said. As for my family being open, I didn't know how to tell him that I *had* showed them the ring in its box but that my parents hadn't seemed to take in its significance. With its free-form modernism setting, it didn't look like an engagement ring to them, I suppose. "Different," my mother had said. "Do you think it's right to accept such a personal gift?" my father asked. "After all, you're only eighteen and have three more years of school." But surely, although all three of us were denying it, they must have known something was up. When I left them at the Portland train station, Mother embarassed me by weeping. She always did that when we said good-bye, but this time it wasn't just misty eyes but great gulping sobs. Father said, "Just don't do anything you wouldn't want to tell me about."

Part of me knew that this was an absurd injunction for my father to burden me with but still, I felt its weight, along with other confusions about what was truly right and wrong.

I wasn't confused at all about Stanford's Honor Code and wouldn't have dreamed of breaking its rule of never giving or receiving unpermitted aid on exams. But its adjunct, the Fundamental Standard, which required that no woman student ever be alone with a male in his place of residence, fell into the category of my father's rules—surely not to be taken seriously. Yet, if the honor code felt cleanly right, for all time, why didn't it follow that The Fundamental Standard was for my own inner good? One didn't choose to obey only the Ten Commandments that were easy.

By the social lights of the fifties, the codifiers of The Fundamental Standard had my number, I realized, one storm-ridden Saturday afternoon. While his housemates attended the Stanford-Army game, I persuaded Jack to listen to the proceedings on the radio at the Hunting Lodge, as he'd dubbed the cabin in Los Trancos Woods.

As the rain pounded on the tar and gravel roof of the Lodge, and the announcer droned on about failed receivers and muddy passes, Jack and I found one of the bottom bunks so alluring, unencumbered as it was by the Studebaker's gear shift and steering wheel, that I heard myself begging my hardworking graduate student to do that which this interminable caressing must lead to. He bolted upright and retreated into a cold shower. As I buttoned and smoothed my disheveled clothes and squeezed my thighs together to ease the ache in my groin, I thought that I never would learn to be as good as my future husband, I the supposed Christian.

It was the Tuesday after this bottoming-out of my moral character that I wrote my parents asking for permission to be married at Christmas, half-way hoping they'd say no and I could go back to being a girl again.

3.
Sex Education

Some years later, my mother told me the story of the day my

letter arrived. Father arrived home from work first and met her at the door with a stiff bourbon on the rocks. "Sit down," he said. "You're going to need this," and handed her my letter.

After reading it, she said she just sat there for a few minutes. Finally she put the letter back in its envelope and asked my father, "What shall we do?"

Father plowed his fingers through his hair, messing the razor-edge part, his usual "I give up" gesture. He gave my mother a sly look. "What do you say we let Jack finish raising her?"

When I phoned my parents on Saturday afternoon to hear their decision, Father answered. Mother was working overtime at the office he told me.

"We got your letter," he said. "What's the big hurry?"

Even across the wires connecting a thousand miles, I was sure he could see my furious blush at his sarcastic tone. It had never occurred to me that he might imagine the reason for our haste was that I could be pregnant. Bitterly I thought: and after I'd been so *good.*

Sweet as pie, I said, "Why there's no hurry at all. Jack just thought we'd both get more studying done if he didn't have to drive back and forth on that windey road to see me. But if you and Mother don't think it's a good idea. . ."

"It's all arranged," Father said. He told me that my mother had reserved the chapel at Trinity Episcopal—"just the family and some of your friends. We can't afford to make a big deal out of this." Her boss had offered to throw a reception at the University Club. Aunt Midge wanted to give me a bridal shower.

He said we'd have to be in Portland in time to get our Wasserman tests processed before the five day waiting period for the license. "And your mother says to hurry up and pick out china and silver patterns. Naturally, she's blabbed it all over town that you're marrying into this fine Medford family and people want to know what to send."

After I hung up I sat for a time in the dorm cubicle gazing at the arrow-stabbed hearts other co-eds had penned on the walls. Silver patterns? Bridal showers? Wasserman tests? I hadn't been reading the right books, I realized, as I made my way to the bookstore for instruction. Only seven weeks to cram for the examinations that lay ahead.

"Lordy all this sounds complicated," I complained to my roommate from my top bunk. Mona was at her desk, conjugating French verbs. "There are so many different positions. 'Posterior-lateral,' 'Suspended,' 'Prone or ventral.' Oh my god: 'equestrian'!"

I thunked my chin down on the bed rail. "Why you'd have to be at it almost day and night just to get through the basics."

Mona, one of six children in a Catholic family, muttered, "Don't worry. I think eventually things ease off."

I'd abandoned Amy Vanderbilt's book on wedding etiquette as too boring and was poring over *Ideal Marriage: Its Physiology and Technique*, by Th. Van de Velde, copyright 1926. "It's considered the classic handbook," the older woman clerk in the bookstore had whispered. "Marriage is a science," the book's preface said, warning that the information contained within was offered "without a scintilla of eroticism and yet with a sustained note of high idealism." The ponderous prose certainly didn't provide any turn-on; in fact, the whole enterprise of sexual congress sounded distinctly icky.

"Get this," I said to Mona. "Here's the advice Empress Maria Theresa's doctor gave her when she consulted him about her sterility. 'I am of the opinion that the clitoris of your Most Sacred Majesty should be titillated for some length of time before coitus.' "

"*Clit*oris," Mona corrected my pronunciation. She'd taken a creampuff course on Marriage and the Family. Which, I now realized was what I should have taken instead of The Modern House. At least now I knew the name for that part of my body that strummed and hummed so inexplicably when Jack's hands touched my breasts.

"Well anyway, it worked. Her Sacred Majesty went on to have eighteen children." I studied the fold-out plate of Woman's Genital Organs. It looked like the mouth of a woman screaming.

"Mona? Where do babies come out of?"

My friend swiveled in her chair and looked up at me. "You mean to tell me that you don't know?"

"Just testing you," I said blithely. In high school, when my mother had asked me if there was anything I needed to know, I told her I'd read all about it in one of my aunt's childbirth books. Somehow I'd misunderstood the pictures. My stupefying naivete had led me to believe that the mother's belly button opened up to release the infant.

My parents wrote that they'd moved from the American Apartments, where I'd grown up, to a newer building overlooking the park blocks. When I arrived home a week before the wedding, I smelled just a whiff of cabbage dinners in the corridors and the rooms of their unit, while small, were light and airy above the park's alders and maples.

"Where's my room?" I asked, looking for a place to put down my suitcase.

Mother, setting the table in the tiny dinette, looked startled. "Why honey, we never could have afforded a two bedroom place. You're getting married. Remember?"

Father was stirring a pot in the kitchen and when my mother squeezed past him to get the salt and pepper, I saw him give her fanny a little pat. Instead of ignoring him, she nudged his leg with her ankle and batted her eyes. I wondered when they'd gotten to be so chummy.

Frostily, I asked, "What did you do with my bed?"

"We sold it," Father said. "No place to store it."

"How about my dolls and that stuff?"

Mother looked anxiously at my father and then back at me. "Honey, you hadn't touched those dolls in years. I gave them to Midge's kids. Now come and look at all the wedding gifts that have come for you and Jack. We can hardly pry our way into our bedroom there's so many."

That night as I lay curled up in the old grey comforter on the living room sofa, with less than startling originality I thought: well, you made your bed, now lie in it. I had to laugh at myself. Had I really expected my old bedroom always to stay intact, waiting for me?

I'd never imagined that on their own, my parents might have a whole new life. Then I remembered that when I was in grade school, sometimes on rainy Sunday afternoons my father would give me a quarter with instructions to walk around the block three times. Somehow he made it seem a vitally important errand and I'd shrug into my hat and coat and trudge out into the rain. It was a long block but I never stinted on three full turns. Now I giggled aloud. So *that's* what that had all been about.

I didn't really mind about the dolls—I never had played much with them. There was one, though, that I was awfully fond of, a boy doll from Finland I'd named Poika. He'd come dressed in felt shorts and a checked shirt and suspenders with the most cunning buttons. Poika's bright blue eyes were painted on his cloth face so that he was always awake, unlike my girl dolls with creepy glass eyes that closed and opened in a dead stare. He always looked so cheerful sitting on my shelf that often I looked up from the book I was reading and winked at him.

At Midge's bridal shower the following evening, I wandered away from the guests exclaiming over the clam dip to say hi to her girls, three mopey, straggly-haired stairstep versions of the same homely child. Their bedroom was a mess of deeply hopeless proportions: lipstick ground into the linoleum rug, jumbled clothes oozing out of the open drawers and closet and a strong ammonia smell. I guessed that one of the little girls was a bedwetter. "Mama says no one's supposed to come in here," the oldest said without spirit. She was spooning cornflakes to a hairy mongrel who was hunkered down on the lower bunk.

Poor Midge with her pert pompadour and swaying hips. I wondered if she foresaw all this that Sunday afternoon during the war when she'd flirted with my uncle at the beer parlor.

I'd never had much rapport with the girls—or children in general, for that matter. "How do you like my dolls?" I asked.

The girls giggled and stared at the dog licking cornflakes from his chops.

"I see," I said levelly. "Now I hope you girls aren't going to make a lot of racket at the wedding."

I also hoped that they'd given Poika a decent burial. I gave the memory of his bright blue eyes an elegaic wink.

When I opened the shower gifts, set after set of Pyrex bowls, Mother kept correcting my faint thank yous. "Our bowls," she said softly. "No more *me* and *my*. Now you say *we* and *our*. All this isn't for you, you're a couple now, remember?"

Midge's package contained a black lace nightgown. "Woo-woo," one of the guests whistled. "That should put him in the mood," another woman crowed. I burst into tears. "Thank you Midge, for my beautiful nightgown," I blubbered.

"Bridal nerves," my grandmother said knowingly. The other women nodded and went back to their sour jokes about their husbands.

That night I tried to write thank you notes back at the new apartment. "Dear Mr. and Mrs. Wentworth," I wrote, "Jack and I just love our sterling silver compote dish. When we get back to school, we plan to have a lot of compote parties..." I tore up the letter.

We could call the whole thing off, I realized. Return the gifts, tell them we'd changed our minds. I'd been fitted for a diaphragm at the Stanford Health Service and really, that was all Jack and I needed for what we both wanted most. It had been shockingly easy to get the diaphragm that would almost guarantee we wouldn't have kids (even though I hadn't succeeded in inserting it by myself yet).

Jack and I could meet secretly at motels. It would be so much more romantic.

But then I conjured up the image of my husband-to-be, once again admired the miracle of his long, straight eyelashes. Curly lashes would have made him too good-looking. And I realized that he was the only person left in the world who promised me abiding love, that essential sustenance I'd so long taken for granted from my parents in their different ways. How brave children are, I thought, to sleep alone.

And I also thought how much trouble it would be to wrap up and mail back all those compote dishes and waffle irons, not to speak of the Pyrex bowls. It was easier, no doubt, just to go ahead and get married.

5.
Until Death Do Us Part

The wedding eve, Mother tucked me into the living room sofa and poured me a warm bourbon and milk. We could hear Father snoring in the bedroom and I sensed her need for some farewell to her only child. Earlier into the day we'd both been embarassed when she'd presented me with a package from the drugstore. "You'll need this," she said. "The directions are inside." It was a douche bag and without comment I tossed the ugly red rubber device into the suitcase that was my temporary home.

While I sipped my toddy in awkward silence, she sat in father's old easy chair, her legs tucked under the cushion.

"Mama," I said finally—I hadn't called her that since I was five—"tell me again how you felt when I was born."

She grinned and slapped her forehead in her "dumb me" gesture. "Oh I was so terrible. I wanted a boy so bad. When they told me you were a girl I just turned my face to the wall. I refused to even look at you.

"Then the next day your Daddy brought me flowers and he said, 'Esther, she's so cute.' He made me walk down to the nursery and pick you up. And you know, you really weren't cute at all. Your eyes were red from the drops they put in and your skin was all flakey.

"But there was something about the way your head bobbled and that soft spot on top. My heart just melted."

"So that's how it begins," I said. "Easy as that."

"Yep," she said. "And it never stops. Not ever."

On my (our) wedding day, a fierce storm whipped the last of the autumn leaves into sodden messes that clung to the stone steps leading to the chapel. Father and I stood in the foyer waiting for the organist's cue. "Now hold tight to my arm," Father said. "I'm so nervous I can't stand it."

I more or less pulled him down the aisle to the strains of "Jesu, Joy of Man's Desiring" and when we got to the altar, Father looked so faint that I tried to hold him up by the sheer force of my stare. Only after the minister had asked who giveth this woman and my father said that he did, did I look at Jack.

For a fraction of a second I saw the man standing there in a double-breasted suit as a stranger, not very tall, the fine hair of his crewcut revealing his scalp; and didn't he show a shade too much of his gums when he smiled? And then the moment passed and once again he was my handsome, cherished friend.

When the minister asked me to repeat "Until death do us part," I was stunned by the enormity of the vow. Tears crowded my eyes and with horror I realized that my nose was running. The minister smiled indulgently as Jack took his perfectly folded handkerchief from his breast pocket and I blew my nose. Then I promised.

When we came out of the chapel, it was raining furiously and as I ran down the steps to the car waiting to take us to the reception, my new pumps slipped from under me and I landed at the bottom in a pile of wet leaves. Jack had me back on my feet in an instant, his face stricken with concern but I was laughing my head off. "They should have put sand on those steps," he said severely. "You could have broken your leg."

"I know," I giggled. "Wouldn't it have been hilarious if after all this, I'd had to spend our wedding night in traction?"

A bride with mud stains on the tulle of her dress somehow gave the reception a buzz of merriment and everyone had a wonderful time, especially me. I was even sweet to Midge's girls who only had one hair-pulling fight. Friends of my Civic Theater and high school days surrounded me and all the good times I'd had in the City of Roses filled my heart with affection. I'd just been handed another glass of champagne and was gossiping with my former drama coach about the actor who played Shylock, when Jack told me it was time to go. I teased to stay a little longer.

With a worried look, he said, "Another storm front is moving in." We were headed for a cabin on the coast.

It was pouring too hard for anyone to come outside and throw rice or wave us goodbye. As we crossed the bridge over the Willamette and away from Portland's shimmering neon, I thought that soon my husband and I would see each other naked for the first time and then we would begin to be truly married. "Wasn't it a perfect wedding?" I asked Jack, patting his knee. There was no answer but the windshield wiper's squeak. I saw from his intent profile that he was concentrating on carrying us safely over the rain-slick highway ahead.

GIVING MY MOTHER A BATH

MID-MORNING of her third day home from the hospital with a new hip, I rig up this contraption in her bathtub—a wooden stool that rests on the pull-out kitchen breadboard for a stable base. In her walker she backs up to the tub and I guide her broad white rump onto the stool. She swings her good leg over the side and down into the easeful water. "Oh my," she sighs. "This feels so fine."

The right leg she can't yet bend sticks out over the rim like a useless oar. I scan the tiny bathroom for a prop—we're too far into this precarious enterprise to quit now. My overnight case I've stashed under the sink looks the right height. With my toe I slide it under her bad leg. If she asked me for some trinket in Tiffany's window, I think I'd smash plate glass with my bare hands to grab it for her. But all she wants is a bath.

Slowly I soap the cloth with Dove. I haven't seen her naked in a long time. "My how you've grown," I say.

She pats her belly-mound. "Let's face it. I am *fat*."

Ever since the arthritic hip began to hurt so much she gave up walking beyond the mailbox on her front porch, her restless energy has focused on eating. She treats every meal like a miracle. A dab of gravy trembling on her chin, she'll declare. "This must be the best food God every put on this earth"; her eyes greedily check the serving dishes for seconds.

I hold up the washcloth. "Where shall we begin?"

She shuts her eyes and thrusts out her homely mug for my lathered blessing. I remember how I squirmed at the rough kiss of her spit on a hankie when she rubbed soot from my cheeks. Now, her brow untroubled, she submits to my soaping; her very pores seem open to whatever may come.

Through the cloth I memorize her face. At seventy-eight, her wrinkles aren't as deeply incised as mine, although compared to the sorrows and hardships she's endured, most of my life has seemed trivially easy. For one thing, I've always had her; she was six when her own mother died.

With my ring finger I pat the pouches under her eyes and smooth the lines that river from the roots of her nose into tiny creeks at the corners of her mouth. I wipe away traces of yesterday's lipstick and feel the lump of calcification that protects a speck of glass buried in her lower lip—on a rainy night ten years ago, she swerved to miss a motorcyclist and went through the windshield of her Buick. The lump gives her mouth, in repose, a stubborn look at odds with her bonny disposition. I have an unforgivable thought: she's going to look angry in her casket.

Under the loose skin of her high cheekbones, I feel the shape of the skull that will survive, as probably somewhere still lie buried the wide-malared skulls of our ancestors who drove herds across central Asia into the Finnish north.

I press the browbones above her eyes, smoothing upward the skimpy hairs she fills in with pencil.

"That feels real good," she says. She thinks I'm giving her a massage. With my other hand, I rub the knot of muscles at the base of her neck. I know exactly how to do it so the nerves cry out with pleasure. Early on, when she rubbed my neck with her big-knuckled fingers in the exact spots where I hurt, I realized that she and I tighten up in all the same places. Even when she sleeps, she doesn't look relaxed but in a hurry.

"You should try and sit up straight." I pull back her shoulders and feel the resistance of the hump her spine is curving toward. Briefly she straightens, sighs "Ah, Gahd," and slumps again, yielding to gravity's seductive tug. I pull back my own shoulders.

"Water too cold?"

"A little," she admits.

"Why didn't you say so?"

She shrugs.

"I'm not going to wash your hair."

"So don't. Big deal," she says.

Before the surgery, Phoebe the beautician gave her an unfortunate "wash & wear" cut—two inches at its longest—and permanented her fine hair into feeble curls that look like the dust kittens under a bed. Now her exposed ears seem enormous.

"Actually, it's kind of cute," I say.

"Thank you very much," she says drily. "Thanks a thousand." Her vanities are unpredictable. "Do you think we could get on with this?"

I soap her neck wattles and bail palmsful of water into the hollows of her mended collarbone. When she was eighteen, she broke it on a forbidden ride in Dexter Johnson's Model T. The steering wheel came off in Dexter's hands. She told me that he gaily kept turning the wheel in thin air as they careened down those washboard country roads singing "Nearer My God to Thee." Until the car smashed into a tree.

Dexter came out fine. She fractured her skull. For a year after, half her face was paralyzed. "God punished me," she says now, as she does every time this story gets told, "for disobeying my father."

"That's horse manure," I tell her.

The paralysis left her with a left eyelid that droops when she's tired and a crooked smile. I have that same smile. For years I believed that acquired traits can be inherited.

Even though he died of t.b. long before I was born, I've always been in love with the Dexter Johnson of this story. Who knows? If the steering column hadn't broken, he might have been my Daddy.

"That Dexter sure had *sisu*," I tell my mother. *Guts* in Finnish. Only more: guts and style.

"Just think. If Dexter Johnson had been my father, I'd be ten years older."

"Sweetie-pie, there's no way Dexter Johnson could have been your father. For one thing, my father would never have let me marry a Swede."

She gives me a mock-prissy toss of her head. "And we didn't *do* it back then, you know. Before marriage."

I doubt that without her bifocals she catches my smile. One thing we never talk about is that I was born less than seven months after my parents' wedding day.

She explained it once: "You were premature."

Seven pounds, six ounces, it says on my birth certificate. Lucky for her I didn't go full term.

I rinse the back of her neck. The new haircut reveals the port wine stain at the nape. I almost forgot that I have the same birthmark—the reason I wear my hair long enough to cover all but a drop of the wine. How can she think it matters that my birth came awkwardly early, when I am so indisputably hers?

Let her have her little secret. I've committed some folly here and there I hope my sons don't know about, or if they do know, have the grace and wits not to let on.

Her bra straps have forced tracks into her fleshy shoulders. I travel down and soap her huge breasts, pulling up their pliant weight to get at the skin over her ribs. Her skin is beautiful; not papery-sad but plumped out with inner shine.

"Boy. I sure am glad I didn't get your boobs," I tease.

She hoots. "Now you're glad. Don't you remember in high school stuffing Kleenex in your bra?"

"I remember when you bought me my first one. Daddy said, 'Will you please tell me why she needs a bra for those little walnuts?' "

She smiles indulgently. "Your father. Wasn't he funny?"

"Hilarious."

"I miss him." With cupped palms, she bounces her breasts a little, as if to give them some exercise before they have to be strapped in again. "Don't you miss him?"

Oh my. A hard question. To me, missing someone means to wish he were here right now, maybe in the next room, the way I miss my dead husband. The last several years of his life, my father was as difficult and manic-crazy as you can get without being locked up. If he were still alive, I doubt that she'd have survived these last five years.

She doesn't know I write stories about my girlhood so I can't tell her that often he comes into them, completely uninvited. I'm always glad to be with him again for awhile. I know exactly what he would say and I faithfully write it down, knowing I can send him away when I need to.

"Sure I miss him," I tell my mother. "But as he would say after Aunt Ida went home after a visit, 'it's a good miss.' "

"I bet you miss Larry," she says. "You poor kid. Having to drop everything to fly up here and work your fingers to the bone."

Larry is the man I live with—rather, who lives with me. When I first introduced him to her as "an old friend from Menlo Park," she was cool. That was the winter before my father's death when she'd had a mild stroke and I snatched her away to San Francisco to recuperate in peace at my place.

When Larry showed up every night at dinnertime, she'd say, "You sure seem to like the food around here, Roy." And when in the morning she found him reading the paper at the breakfast table: "Back so soon from Menlo Park, Earl?"

Then one day for no particular reason—except that perhaps she saw that he made me happy—she decided to love him. As is her style in that department, she didn't go halfway

"It's funny," she muses now. "I think I loved Jack—God-rest-his-darling-soul—more than any mother-in-law ever loved a son-in-law. And now I do believe I love Larry just as much."

"You love everybody," I complain, a spoiled child still wanting to be her mother's only miracle. I've reached the nether of her belly and, suddenly dizzy from the steam or from bending, I hand over the washcloth.

"You do your *takapuoli* and your privates." I shunt around her walker and sit on the lid of the hospital-supply commode that elevates the toilet. While she obediently washes the mysterious and unspeakable regions from which I sprang, I stare at the stippled pink of the ceiling. It needs a coat of paint.

She waves the cloth to show she's finished her assignment. On my knees, I address the less complicated expanse of her back.

Two years ago the cancerous lobe of one lung was removed. Now the scar under her left shoulder blade is an almost imperceptible line, as if someone simply had run his fingernail across her flesh. I still regret that I couldn't come take care of her then. Her younger sister, the humorless and dutiful Ida, bussed down from Spokane. She'll come again in a few days when I have to leave.

"So what are you going to do to devil Aunt Ida this time?" The last convalescence, her sister lectured her so relentlessly about cigarettes causing the cancer that my mother, although she'd lost all nicotine-craving during her long hospital stay, forced herself to chain-smoke in Ida's presence.

"It almost killed me, but I did it," she told me on the phone when she reported that Ida had fled home in tears on the Greyhound.

"*Gahd*, that Ida," she says now. She scrooches up her face. "Can't you stay and spare me?"

"You know you love Aunt Ida."

She puts on her stubborn look. "Of course I love her. I just can't stand her."

The neat new scar on her lower back, where just three weeks ago another surgeon cut in and broke her hip to install the artificial one, looks almost healed. For comparison, I pull down the waistband of my jeans and show her my jagged forty-year-old appendix scar.

"See? Yours already looks better."

She clucks over my scar. "You poor kid. Back then they kept you a whole month in the hospital. You cried so hard when I left after visiting hours that I'd come home and cry all night."

I massage the nest of nerves on her tailbone. "I wasn't crying for you. I was weeping for my sins."

Between grunts of pleasure at what I'm doing to her coccyx, she says, "That's ridiculous. You've never sinned in your life. You were born perfect and you stayed that way."

"Oh I sinned all right. I lied about having a stomachache because I wanted to get out of my arithmetic class." To this day I associate long division with the smell of gas and post-operative retching.

"What are you talking about? You were a very sick girl."

I slosh water on her back and on my knees move around the overnight case to work on the foot that's in the water.

"My big mistake was saying the pain was on my right side. How was I to know that's where your appendix is?—I was only in fifth grade. Before I knew it, there I was in St. Vincent's with a scalpel poised over my perfect innards."

She grabs my wrist so fiercely I drop the cloth; with her other hand she takes my chin so I have to look her in the eye.

"Do you mean to tell me there was nothing wrong with you? Dr. Essex said your appendix was going to burst and you might die."

I try and reach back for how all this came about—it's been a long time.

"You had *Forever Amber* from the rental library hidden in your top drawer." She rarely took time to read books but everyone was talking about this one; and it had been denounced by the Methodist Board of Temperance and Morals which made it irresistible.

"I could tell from the bookmark that you were almost finished. And so I told the teacher I had this godawful stomachache so I could read how it turned out while you were at work. It cost ten cents a day—you were sure to return it the next morning."

She drops my wrist. "Well I'll be damned. I always thought that doctor with his Thomas Dewey moustache was a horse's *takapuoli*." She breathes hard. "Why didn't you say you were faking? I would have believed you and put a stop to it."

I fish the cloth out of the scummy water and work on her hammertoes. The water has softened her corns and callouses;

if I had a pumice stone handy, I probably could scour them away.

There's really no answer to her question. I'm in no mood now to blame my ten-year-old self for moral cowardice. Or on the other hand to give her much credit for accepting the radical consequences of her lie. Losing my appendix without cause just happened. Like so many human events that later take on emotional cargo, things had gone too far before I realized it *was* an event; and that I was trapped in it.

My mother rubs her brow with the heel of her hand. "I feel terrible—that you went through all that for nothing. I feel so guilty."

"If anyone, that rat-snout doctor should feel guilty." I pinch her big toe. "You've never done a single thing in your life you should feel guilty about."

Her left eye twitches. "You don't know half of it. It makes me sick that I worked when you were little. That you spent all that time alone in the apartment, growing up without brothers and sisters. And then about your father...."

"I'm the one who should feel guilty about him. And you would have been bored silly staying home. It just so happens, I had a wonderful childhood." As soon as I say it, I realize that it's true. How tedious it would have been to grow up in a bland steady family like the one depicted in my first grade primer.

She gives a sad little laugh. "You can't understand because you're only half-Finnish. By nature, a Finlander is born feeling guilty. You tell us to jump, we ask, 'how high?' "

"Mother, I hate to disappoint you, but the Finns did not invent guilt."

"Yah? So who did?"

"I don't know. The Jews, I suppose. Moses and that crowd."

She sighs. "I guess I must be Jewish then."

"It's what I've always suspected. Let's face it—how many Methodists do you know with a decent sense of humor?"

"Aren't you *funny*," she chides. "Just like your father."

"You have beautiful feet," I tell her.

"Are you kidding? I hate my ugly feet."

"Don't you dare hate those feet. Do you realize all they've done for you?"

I think of when she was a girl lonely for her mother and her feet carried her through the mud morning and night to milk the cows; the hand-me-down shoes they squeezed into; how they ran away to Seattle to escape her father's sin-obsessed Calvinism; the steps they've climbed; the errands for others they've run; when her hip heals, the heavy weight they still will bear.

"Praise these feet," I declaim, giving her a good show with the broad gestures I learned years ago in drama school. I plant a kiss on her unwashed foot that sticks out over the tub. "May these feet clump on forever!"

"Cut that out," she says, embarrassed. "Sometimes I swear you act as crazy as your father. Trying to make me feel guilty for insulting my dumb feet. Honestly."

I see how tired she is. Her breathing sounds like a mushy piston and her left eye droops at half-mast. She's clean enough, I decide, and I ease her good leg over the side of the tub and swaddle her in fluffy towels.

But when I try and hoist her from the stool, she's dead weight. Three times I try. Her arms clasped around my neck, she grunts and strains to help.

"Oh God," she cries out in anger. "How did I get so old?"

"Give me a minute," I say. "I'll think of something."

I sit on the commode. Patiently, her lower lip looking stubborn, she stares at the bathroom wall. The leaky faucet drips fresh water into the tub. No doubt the breadboard's warping away down there and will never fit back into its slot—what a dumb idea that was.

But my mind isn't puzzling the present problem. I've gone far back to when I used to sit on the toilet lid to be near her while she bathed before going to work.

She was thin then. Her full breasts rode high above the water line. Her lovely lopsided grin revealed her own teeth. When she kissed me goodbye, she smelled of Blue Grass, not the faint, dank vapors of age. She was never sick. And she was never, ever going to die.

Now she clears her throat. "I hate to tell you this"—she rolls her eyes with clownish urgency—"but I have to go to the *hysikka.*"

"Mama, I don't know what to do." I can't even get her out of the tub, much less over to the toilet.

"You go out. Leave me alone. I can manage if I don't have to worry about you worrying."

"You might fall." She absolutely must not fall. The new hip could pop out of its socket like a boomerang.

"Am-scray," she says. "Right now."

I pick up the overnight case and push her walker closer to the tub and close the door behind me. From the hall I listen to her hum the first eight bars of "The Last Time I Saw Paris," over and over, the way she does when she's intent on a task. There's a couple of minor clunks, like plastic bottles falling on tile; when I hear the steady stream of her passing water, the sighs of her relief, I turn away from my cautionary eavesdropping and go into her room and turn down the bed.

After I hear the toilet flush, I give her a few minutes before I open the door. She wears the fresh blue nightie I had ready and, standing in her walker, she's busy teasing up her dust-kittens. Now that my eyes have adjusted, I decide the haircut really is pretty cute.

"How did you manage all that?" I help her maneuver the walker around the tight corner into her bedroom.

She looks terribly pleased with herself. "Oh I'm a tough old turkey. If you'd given me more time, I'd have scoured out my ring instead of leaving it for you."

She backs into her bed and I swing her legs up and arrange the sponge block under her thighs. This part I'm getting pretty good at. Her cheek burrows into the pillow and when I pull up the coverlet she sighs with happiness and closes her eyes.

I ask her what she wants for lunch.

Slyly, she opens one eye. "What do Jewish people like to eat?"

"How about gravlax on Swedish rye?"

She makes smacking noises with her lips.

"Hey. I could schlep down to Safeway and pick up a bottle of Manischevitz."

"Whatever," sleepily she says.

"See you later."

My hand is on the doorknob when she says, "Wait a minute. I have to ask you. Something's been bothering me."

I think, here it comes: some small truth I later can take out and hold up to the light. "Now I'll tell you about my mother," I'll say to my grandchildren once they're born and old enough to be interested.

"Tell me," I say.

Her eyes stay closed. "Did you ever find out how *Forever Amber* ends?"

I give this matter some thought. "I guess not. When I left her, things looked dark. The king was sore at her and she was coming down with the pox—poor Amber." I don't say that I've reached an age where I don't need to know how some stories turn out.

"Don't worry," she says. "I remember it perfectly. It's hilarious the way she escapes to America. You'll laugh, I promise. Fix lunch now. When I wake up, I'll tell you all about it." And with at least one debt settled for now, she hurries off into the aloneness of her sleep.